Eyewitness
MUMMY

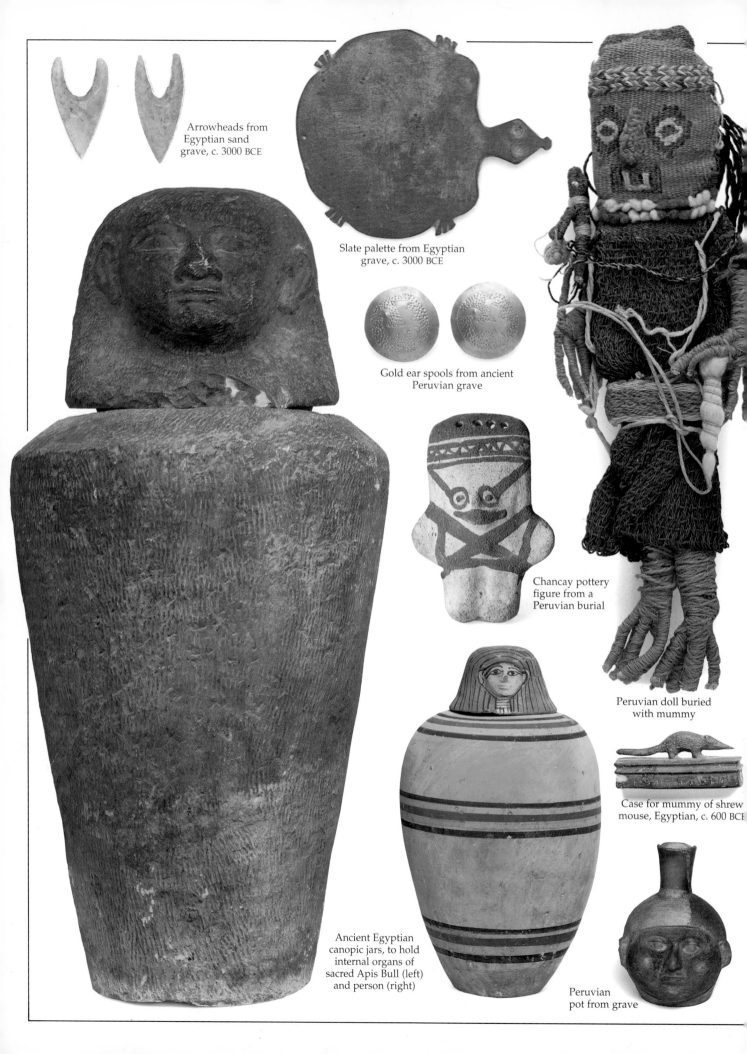

Arrowheads from
Egyptian sand
grave, c. 3000 BCE

Slate palette from Egyptian
grave, c. 3000 BCE

Gold ear spools from ancient
Peruvian grave

Chancay pottery
figure from a
Peruvian burial

Peruvian doll buried
with mummy

Case for mummy of shrew
mouse, Egyptian, c. 600 BCE

Ancient Egyptian
canopic jars, to hold
internal organs of
sacred Apis Bull (left)
and person (right)

Peruvian
pot from grave

Wooden figure
of Anubis, the
ancient
Egyptian god
of embalming

Eyewitness
MUMMY

Hand from ancient
Egyptian mummy
with individually
wrapped fingers

Written by
JAMES PUTNAM

Photographed by
PETER HAYMAN

Wooden face from
ancient Egyptian
mummy case

Magical amulets with heads
of four sons of Horus

DK
DK Publishing, Inc.

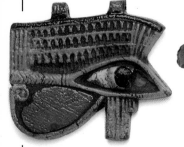

Flint knife found in ancient Egyptian grave, c. 3000 BCE

Fist amulet

Wedjat-eye amulet

DK

LONDON, NEW YORK, MELBOURNE,
MUNICH, and DELHI

Project editor Scott Steedman
Art editor Bob Gordon
Managing editor Helen Parker
Managing art editor Julia Harris
Production Louise Barratt
Picture research Cynthia Hole
Editorial consultants The Department of Egyptian
Antiquities, British Museum

REVISED EDITION
Managing editor Andrew Macintyre
Managing art editor Jane Thomas
Senior editor Kitty Blount
Senior art editor Martin Wilson
Editor and reference compiler Susan Malyan
Art editor Rebecca Johns
Production Jenny Jacoby
Picture research Sarah Pownall

U.S. editor Elizabeth Hester
Senior editor Beth Sutinis
Art director Dirk Kaufman
U.S. DTP designer Milos Orlovic
U.S. production Chris Avgherinos

This Eyewitness ® Guide has been conceived by
Dorling Kindersley Limited and Editions Gallimard

This edition published in the United States in 2004
by DK Publishing, Inc.
375 Hudson Street, New York, NY 10014

04 05 06 07 08 10 9 8 7 6 5 4 3 2 1

Copyright © 1988, © 2004, Dorling Kindersley Limited

A catalog record for this book is
available from the Library of Congress.

ISBN 0-7566-0707-8 (HC) 0-7566-0706-X (Library Binding)

Color reproduction by
Colourscan, Singapore
Printed in China by Toppan Printing Co.
(Shenzhen), Ltd.

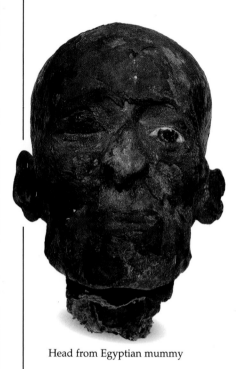

Head from Egyptian mummy

Chimu
mummy
bundle

Discover more at

www.dk.com

Gilded wooden coffin
of ancient Egyptian
priestess, c. 1250 BCE

Contents

Egyptian pot containing
linen mummy bandages,
c. 2000 BCE

What are mummies?

MUMMIES ARE THE PRESERVED BODIES of people or animals. The word was first used to describe the bandaged bodies of ancient Egyptians. But any dead body that still has skin on it is a mummy. If people die or are buried in the right conditions, they may be mummified (preserved) by accident (pp. 8–9). This can happen in wet, marshy places (pp. 58–59) or in the freezing cold of mountains or the polar regions. But most often, people are preserved by being dried out. Many cultures have developed a chemical process – called embalming – to achieve this artificially. The ancient Egyptians are famous for their skillful embalming and their elaborate burial customs. But people all over the world have embalmed their dead. Wherever it is practiced, mummification is usually done for religious reasons. Most cultures believe in some kind of afterlife (life after death). By preserving a dead person's body in recognizable form, they hope to prepare him or her for a better future life.

STUFFED ANIMALS
Unlike mummies, stuffed animals are usually little more than dried skin complete with feathers or fur. The taxidermist props this up with a wire framework to make a lifelike animal.

WHY MUMMY?
Egyptian mummies were coated in dark resins. When Arabs invaded Egypt in the 7th century A.D., they thought this was bitumen (asphalt) and called them *mummiya* – Arabic for bitumen.

OUR LEADER
Famous people are sometimes mummified. The Russian revolutionary leader Vladimir Lenin was preserved using a secret technique that involved paraffin wax. Millions of people have traveled to Moscow to see his body lying in state in Red Square.

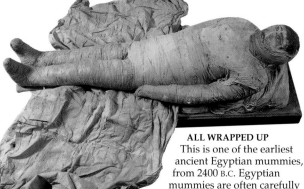

ALL WRAPPED UP
This is one of the earliest ancient Egyptian mummies, from 2400 B.C. Egyptian mummies are often carefully wrapped in hundreds of feet of linen bandages (pp. 16–17).

INTO THE AFTERLIFE
The Egyptians believed that a person's soul left the body at death (pp. 12–13). After the burial, the soul was reunited with the body, and the mummy lived on in the afterlife. For all this to happen, the body had to be well preserved. Then it was bandaged and laid in a coffin or mummy case. The technique of embalming developed gradually over ancient Egypt's long history. It reached its peak around 1000 B.C., but Romans living in Egypt were still being mummified in the third century A.D. (pp. 42–43). This well-wrapped mummy of a 50-year-old man probably dates from the Late Period, between 715 and 332 B.C.

False beard

Mummy wrapped in linen bandages

Base of mummy case

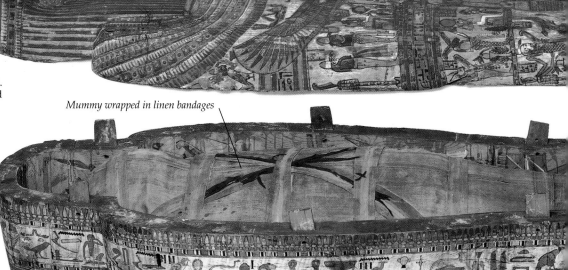

MUMMIFIED BUDDHA

Certain Buddhist priests in Japan practiced mummification. The mummies were set up in temples and worshipped like statues. The priests who became mummies were given the title *Sokushin-butsu*, which means "a Buddha of the body." This is the priest Tetsuryukai. He participated in his own mummification by eating a special grain-free diet for the three years before he died, in 1868. Then the other priests smoke-dried his body with huge candles.

STOPPING THE ROT

Ancient Egyptian embalmers realized that a body's internal organs were the first to decay. So they removed the lungs, liver, stomach, and intestines through an incision in the left side (pp. 14–15). The brain was usually extracted through the nose. The empty body could then be dried out by covering it in natron, a naturally occurring salt. Embalm literally means "in balsam," a sweet-smelling oil. After they had been dried, Egyptian mummies were coated in ointments, oils, and resins, to keep the skin supple and lifelike.

Mummy case lid

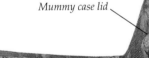

Painted figures of gods

Hooded parka made of sealskin

NICE HAIR

This skull from a female Egyptian mummy dates from around 1600 B.C. As sometimes happens, the flesh has decayed but the tougher hair has been preserved.

THE MUMMY'S HOUSE

Egyptian mummies were usually buried in tombs. In the Old Kingdom (2686–2160 B.C.), the pharaohs (Egyptian kings) built pyramid tombs. These are the famous pyramids at Giza. The largest of the three, the Great Pyramid of Khufu, was made of 2,300,000 blocks of stone and stands 480 ft (146 m) high. Because the mummies were buried inside with many treasures, the pyramids were robbed in ancient times.

ESKIMO BOY

This six-month-old Inuit (Eskimo) boy died around 1475. He is one of eight well-preserved mummies discovered on a jagged cliff in Greenland in 1972. Following Inuit tradition, he had been dressed in warm clothes and left with objects to help him in the next world. Protected from the sun and snow by a rocky overhang, the boy's body was slowly freeze-dried by the cold Arctic air (p. 63).

GOLDEN PHARAOH

Probably the best known pharaoh is Tutankhamun (pp. 38–39). He was not an important ruler, but his intact tomb, found in 1922, was crammed with beautiful treasures. This is his mummy mask, made of solid gold. Compared to that of many pharaohs, his mummy was in poor condition.

Natural mummies

Some of the most remarkable mummies have been preserved by accident. Natural mummies are usually found in extreme climates where dry sands or freezing cold have somehow stopped the process of decay. Decay is caused by bacteria, which breed in the water that makes up over 70 percent of a person's body weight. Hot desert sands can preserve a body by dehydrating it (drying it out). Bodies buried in the icy polar regions may be so thoroughly frozen that decay never starts. Occasionally, bodies have been freeze-dried by a combination of cold temperatures and very dry winds, as found in some mountain caves (pp. 7, 63). In northern Europe, the unusual conditions found in marshy bogs have also preserved bodies remarkably well.

Flint knife buried in sand with body

GRAVE GOODS
All over the world, the dead are buried with beautiful objects. They are usually put there for religious reasons. This 5,000-year-old pot was part of a sand burial. It was meant to hold food the dead person would need in the afterlife.

Dry skin stretched tightly over skeleton

Knees pulled up against chest

SAND MUMMY
The earliest surviving Egyptian mummies date from around 3200 B.C. This is just before the first written records, so very little is known about them. The dead person was placed in a simple grave that was little more than a shallow oval dug in the desert sand. The body lay in a crouched position, with the head to the south and the face turned to the west, toward the setting sun. It was then covered in sand, which mummified it naturally. The many objects buried with the "sand mummies" show that the Egyptians already believed in life after death. The rough graves must have been soon lost in the desert's moving sands, and uncovering such lifelike bodies by accident may have encouraged the Egyptians' beliefs. The most famous sand mummy is nicknamed "Ginger" because of his red hair. This female mummy, also in the British Museum, is known as "Gingerella."

Slate palette in shape of turtle

ADORNING THE BODY
The most curious items found with sand burials were slate palettes. They were used to grind up make-up, and also had an unknown magical function. Necklaces of beads and shells have also been found.

Necklaces of beads and shells

BODY CAST

Over 2,000 ancient Romans died in A.D. 79 when the town of Pompeii was engulfed by a huge eruption of Mount Vesuvius. The volcanic ash set around their bodies like wet cement. Over the years, the bodies decayed, and the ash turned to solid rock. A perfect mold of the body shape survived. When the ruins of Pompeii were excavated, these body hollows were discovered and a method of filling them with liquid plaster was developed. This created a perfect replica of the dead person, like a mummy with flesh of plaster.

Trace of clothing wrapped around body

TOLLUND MAN

This is the head of a man discovered in the Tollund Bog in Denmark in 1950. He has been dead for more than 2,000 years, but looks like he is just sleeping. He was found with a noose around his neck; he is thought to have been sacrificed and thrown into the bog as part of a spring fertility ritual (pp. 58–59).

Sheepskin cap tied under the chin

Noose

Stubble, thought to be two or three days' growth

ICY GRAVE

This is John Torrington, one of three well-preserved mummies discovered by scientists in the Canadian Arctic in 1984. They were English sailors who had died on Sir John Franklin's tragic expedition to find the Northwest Passage. Franklin left England with two ships in 1845, and was never seen again. "It's as if he's just unconscious," marveled one of the scientists as he lifted Torrington from his icy coffin.

BUILDER'S SACRIFICE

Mummies of animals are sometimes found in ordinary houses. Cold drafts of air may freeze-dry the bodies of mice that die in walls or under floorboards. In 16th- and 17th-century England, builders who had almost finished a house used to place a dead animal in a nook somewhere and board it up with a few lucky items. This is a mummified chicken, found behind a brick wall in a 17th-century house in London.

A land lost in time

THE ANCIENT EGYPTIANS went to great lengths to preserve their bodies and their worldly possessions. This has helped the world to rediscover ancient Egypt. The civilization of the pharaohs flourished by the Nile River for over 3,000 years. But until the French invaded Egypt in 1798, it had been largely forgotten. The travelers who visited the country were amazed by its ancient monuments and tombs covered in mysterious hieroglyphics (picture-writing). People have been reopening tombs in search of treasures since ancient times. But until recently, they paid little attention to the mummies. We now know that with the help of modern science, these timeless bodies can tell us amazing things about life and death in the ancient land.

OLD KING'S TOMB
The period we call ancient Egyp began around 3000 B.C. The ste pyramid at Saqqara was built c. 2650 B.C., in the Old Kingdom This was followed by the Midd and New Kingdoms, the Late Period, and then an era when Egypt was ruled by the Greeks and later the Romans.

LANDS OF THE NILE
Egypt is mostly desert, and life has always been concentrated along the banks of the Nile River. In ancient times the land was often divided in two. The northern part, which included the fertile Nile Delta, was called Lower Egypt. In the south was Upper Egypt, which included a large area now flooded by the huge Aswan Dam.

TOMB GUARD
Beautiful statues were placed in tombs for religious reasons. This painted wooden statue represents the god Anubis. He has the head of a jackal, or wild dog. Anubis was the god of mummification and guardian of the cemeteries.

Texture of tigh linen bandage. impressed on ski

NEST FOR A MUMMY
After it was embalmed and wrapped, the mummy was laid in a coffin. This might be the first in a whole series (or nest) of mummy cases. The Egyptians believed these cases would magically protect the body. They were covered in elaborate paintings and spells to help the mummy's spirit on its difficult path through the afterlife.

FAMILIAR FACE?
The ancient Egyptians took extra care preserving the features of the face. This was because they believed the dead person's spirit had to return to the tomb and recognize its body before the mummy could live forever (pp. 12–13).

NAPOLEON MEETS A MUMMY
The French were the first Europeans to study ancient Egypt seriously. When Napoleon Bonaparte invaded Egypt in 1798, he brought a team of scholars and artists with him. Napoleon was fascinated by the ancient land and collected several mummies himself.

ANCIENT LIVES

The ancient Egyptians decorated the walls of tombs with beautiful paintings that tell us a lot about their everyday lives. Paintings that show people farming, hunting, feasting, relaxing, and attending religious and royal ceremonies have all been found.

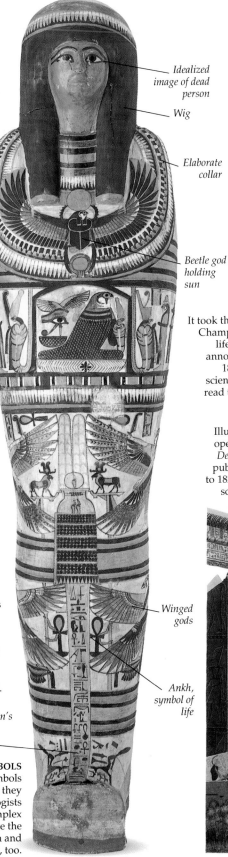

Idealized image of dead person

Wig

Elaborate collar

Beetle god holding sun

Winged gods

Ankh, symbol of life

Spell for dead person's soul written in hieroglyphics

MUMMY TRADE

Excavating in Egypt's hot, dusty climate is tiring. This is a dig in the 1900s. By then, mummies could be sold for a high price. In the 16th and 17th centuries, they were ground up and used in medicines (p. 40). Local people also used them as fuel, as they are soaked in resins and burn well.

FATHER OF EGYPTOLOGY

It took the French scholar Jean-François Champollion (1790–1832) most of his life to decipher hieroglyphics. He announced his first breakthrough in 1822. This allowed Egyptologists, scientists who study ancient Egypt, to read the inscriptions on statues, tombs, temples, and mummy cases.

Illustration from the opening page of *The Description of Egypt*, published from 1809 to 1822 by the team of scholars who went with Napoleon.

TIME CAPSULE

Inside the wrappings of this mummy is a middle-aged Roman man. X-rays show that he suffered from arthritis of the spine (pp. 48–51).

STRANGE SYMBOLS

Mummy cases are covered in religious symbols meant to help the dead person. Only when they could read hieroglyphics could Egyptologists begin to make sense of the Egyptians' complex religious beliefs. The writings often give the name and title of the dead person and sometimes his or her father or mother, too.

The Egyptian Book of the Dead

I T'S CALLED A BOOK, but the Egyptian Book of the Dead is really a collection of magic spells. By about 1400 B.C., they were usually written on a roll of papyrus, the Egyptians' form of paper. There were over 200 spells, which the Egyptians called "The Spells for Coming Forth by Day." Each spell was a prayer or a plea from the dead person, and was meant to help on the difficult voyage to the next world. The ancient Egyptians believed every person had several spirit forms, the most important being the *Ka* and the *Ba*. The *Ka* was the vital energy of life. Like any living thing, the *Ka* needed food and drink, which the Egyptians provided through offerings or images of food placed in the tomb (p. 31). A person's character and ability to move around was called their *Ba*. The *Ba* is something like our idea of a person's spirit or soul, and was usually pictured as a bird. For a person to live forever, his or her *Ba* and *Ka* had to be reunited in the tomb with the mummy. Once this happened, the mummy became an immortal (or *Akh*).

HARD-WORKING SPELL
Shabti figures (pp. 32–33) are painted with a spell promising they will work for the dead person in the afterlife.

GOLD HEART
This gold heart scarab is an amulet (pp. 20–21) worn by the mummy for protection. It is inscribed with a spell to help the heart when it was weighed. An ancient papyrus records that robbers brought to trial in 1125 B.C. confessed that they had stolen it from the tomb of Pharaoh Sobkemsaf II.

HOVERING BA
This *Ba* bird comes from the famous Book of the Dead drawn by the scribe Ani. It went with a spell meant to unite the *Ba* with its mummy.

FIRST BOOKS
In the Old Kingdom, over 4,000 years ago, magic spells were inscribed on the inner walls of pyramids. By the Middle Kingdom, they were painted inside coffins, like this one from 2000 B.C. The first Book of the Dead on papyrus dates from around 1400 B.C.

RISE, MUMMY!
Ba birds have human heads. This little statue was probably originally attached to the foot of a mummy case. The *Ba* is raising its arms, as if it is telling the mummy's spirit to rise. Two outstretched human arms were the hieroglyphic symbol for the *Ka*.

Set of tools used in the
Opening of the Mouth

*Forked tool used to
touch mummy's face*

*Adz, a
tool held up to
mummy's face*

OPEN UP
During the funeral, the
mummy went through
an important ritual
called the Opening of
the Mouth. The ancient
Egyptians believed this
would restore the
mummy's senses, so it
could eat, drink, and enjoy
the afterlife properly. This
illustration is from the Book
of the Dead by the scribe
Hunefer, from c. 1310 B.C.

*Priest in leopard skin
burning incense*

*Food
offerings*

Priests

Mourners

Mummy

JACKAL HEAD
This Anubis mask has a
moving jaw. It may have
been worn by a priest
during rituals like the
Opening of the Mouth.

Priest wearing Anubis mask

*Jury of gods sits
in judgment*

God Osiris

WEIGHING THE HEART
The most important
moment in a mummy's
"life" was the weighing
of its heart. In this
ceremony, a jury of gods
decided whether the
mummy had behaved
well enough on earth to
deserve eternal life. This
was calculated by
weighing the mummy's
heart against a feather,
the symbol of truth. The
jackal god Anubis
performed the ceremony,
and Thoth, the scribe
god, took notes. If sins on
Earth had made the
mummy's heart too
heavy, it was thrown to
the monster Ammit, who
devoured it. But if the
heart balanced with the
Feather of Truth, the
mummy had passed the
test and would live
forever.

*Dead man watches
anxiously with wife*

Ba bird

Heart

*Anubis, the jackal
god, keeps eye on scales*

Feather of Truth

*Thoth, the scribe god,
writes down result*

*Monster Ammit with crocodile's
head waits to devour heart*

BOOK HOLDER
This wooden statue of Osiris, the god
of rebirth (pp. 34–35), was placed in a
tomb. It has a secret compartment
where the Book of the Dead
was hidden.

Base

*Roll of
papyrus*

*Secret
compartment*

EGYPTIAN PAPER
The scribes, ancient
Egypt's full-time
writers, usually copied
the Book of the Dead
onto papyrus. This reed
used to grow in marshes
by the Nile. Strips of
papyrus were woven
together and beaten to form
long rolls like paper.

Making a mummy

Wooden jackal, representing Anubis, the god of embalming

"MY CORPSE IS PERMANENT, it will not perish nor be destroyed in this land for ever." So ends spell 154 in the Book of the Dead (pp. 12–13). From the earliest sand burials 5,000 years ago (p. 8), the Egyptians could see that a body had to be dried to stop it from rotting away. They developed a method of drying with natron, a natural salt that left a corpse more flexible and lifelike than drying with hot sand. Natron absorbs water. It also dissolves body fats, and is a mild antiseptic that kills destructive bacteria. Embalming traditionally took 70 days, of which 40 used to dry the body. But first of all the vital organs, which decay the fastest, had to be removed. Only the heart, which the mummy would need when it was judged in the next world (p. 13), was left. The body was then washed with palm wine and spices and covered in natron. Later, molten (liquid) resin, taken from trees, was poured over the body to help preserve it. To stop it from cracking, the skin was rubbed with a mixture of cedar oil, wax, natron, and gum. Then the body was packed with wads of linen, sand, or even sawdust, to give it shape. Finally the mummy was ready to be wrapped in layers of linen bandages.

EMBALMING EYEWITNE
The Greek historian Herodotus visit Egypt in 450 B.C. and wrote the on eyewitness account of embalming. "In t best treatment," he observed, "first of they draw out the brains through t nostrils with an iron hook…. Next th make an incision in the flank with a sha obsidian blade through which they c extract all the internal organs. Then th clean out the body cavity, rinsing it wi palm wine…(then) they cover the corp with natron for seventy days, but for longer, and so mummify it. After t seventy days are up they wash the corp and wrap it from head to t in bandages of the fine linen anointed with gum

FOUR DUMMIES
The mummy's internal organs were embalmed separately By about 2000 B.C., they were placed in containers called canopic jars. These litt coffins had heads, eith of gods or the dead person. By 1000 B.C., th wrapped organs were put back in the mummy But dummy canopic jar with nothing in them were still put in the tom These dummy jars have the heads of the four gods known as the Sons of Horus (p. 20).

Imsety, with a person's head, guarded the liver

Qebehsenuef, a falcon, held the intestines

Hapy, a baboon, kept an eye on the lungs

Duamutef, a jackal, guarded the stomach

Body / Embalmers pour water from jugs

Body, black from oils and resins, is purified with streams of water

Embalmers / Head embalmer wearing Anubis mask

Lying on bier (couch), body is covered in dry crystals of natron

CANOPIC CHEST

This wooden chest belonged to a doctor called Gua, who died c. 2050 B.C. It contains his four canopic jars. They have human heads – it wasn't until 1500 B.C. that the Sons of Horus (p. 20) became common as stoppers.

Wooden stoppers

Jars made of the stone calcite

BRAIN HOOKS

A rod was usually pushed up the nose to punch a hole into the skull. Then bronze hooks or spoons could be poked in to scoop out the brain.

Head support

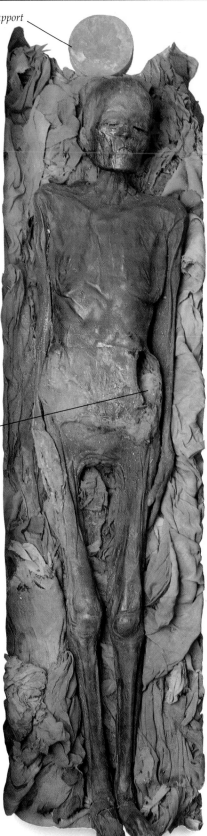

Embalming incision

BOWL OF NATRON

A natural salt, natron was found around the edges of desert lakes near Cairo.

Wax embalming plate with wedjat-eye decoration

Ritual knife with gold handle and flint blade

EMBALMING TOOLS

The embalming incision was usually made on the left side of the body. Herodotus says the knife blade was made of obsidian, a kind of volcanic glass that had to be imported from Ethiopia. But all the ritual knives that have been found have blades of flint. After the organs had been removed, the incision was covered by a plate decorated with a wedjat eye (p. 20).

WHERE THE SUN SETS...

Cemeteries, tombs, and embalmers' workshops were usually on the west bank of the Nile. The Egyptians believed this desert area where the sun set every evening was the land of the dead.

TEP BY STEP
he best pictures
f embalming are
ainted on the
ummy case of
jedbastiufankh,
om about 600 B.C.
his case is now in
e Hildesheim
useum, Germany.

Wrapped mummy

Canopic jars

Mummy, bandaged and wearing a mask (pp. 18–19), is attended by Anubis

WELL PRESERVED

Considering that she was mummified after 600 B.C., around the time Herodotus visited Egypt, this woman has been remarkably well embalmed. By then, the empire was collapsing and the art of embalming was in decline. Embalmers still made sure the mummy looked good on the outside, but they didn't bother much with the insides. Usually bodies were simply coated from head to toe in resin.

Wrapping up

Gold ring

NEED A HAND?
Each finger on this 3,000-year-old mummified hand has been individually wrapped. It is wearing a gold ring set with a scarab beetle (p. 44). Rings and other jewelry were often specially made just to be worn by mummies.

H UNDREDS OF YARDS OF LINEN were used to carefully wrap a mummy. The linen didn't just come in the well-known rolls of bandages. Mummies were also wrapped in shrouds, large sheets of material that were thrown over the body like a cape. Each shroud had to be long enough to be knotted at the top, behind the mummy's head, and also underneath the feet. As many as 20 alternating layers of bandages and shrouds have been counted on one mummy. The exact arrangement of the rolls and shrouds of linen varied a lot from period to period, and can be helpful in dating mummies. The first layer was usually a shroud. Then each finger and toe was wrapped up separately. Next a long strip of linen beginning at the right shoulder was crisscrossed over the head. To hold the head up, a strap was then passed under the chin and knotted on top of the head. As more bandages were added, they were kept very tight, to maintain the mummy's distinctive shape. Protective amulets (pp. 20–21) and sometimes the dead person's jewelry were placed between the layers. At the same time the linen was constantly brushed with sticky, liquid resin. This glued the bandages together and made them slowly stiffen as they dried. Around 15 days were set aside for the wrapping, and the whole process was accompanied by much prayer and ritual.

THE FINAL SHROUD
The wrapping was completed by shroud. This covered the entire mummy and was held in place by a long bandage running from head to toe and crossed by horizontal bands.

Inscription in hieroglyphic

SHROUD FRAGMENT
Numbers had many meanings to the ancient Egyptians. Traditionally, mummies were wrapped in seven shrouds, as this was a magical number. The outer shroud was often painted with magical writings and spells to protect the mummy within.

IT'S A WRAP
In this imaginative picture of a wrapping, an assistant is busy pouring the resin used to hold the bandages together. Lying on a special bier (couch), the mummy is being wrapped in stages, supervised by the chief embalmer. Priests kneel at the feet of the mummy, reciting sacred spells. In the background, more assistants are trying to get the mummy case (pp. 22–27) down the stairs.

OVERSEEING THE MYSTERIES
A special embalmer called the Overseer of Mysteries chose the pieces of linen to go on the head. The eye sockets were covered by pads of linen, and strips were plastered over the face.

Jaw bone

Hair

HAIR MAGIC
A lost hair could be used against the mummy if it fell into enemy hands. So the dead person's hair was gathered together and laid in the tomb with the mummy.

Final
shroud

*Writing used
to date linen*

LINEN OF YESTERDAY

All the wrappings above were unrolled from the
same mummy. The linen varies a lot in quality. The
cheapest was old household cloth. This explains a sad
Egyptian funeral song in which the dead person is said to be
sleeping in the "cast-off linen of yesterday." This domestic
linen is well worn and has often been darned. The best
mummy wrappings were clothes used to dress
statues of gods in the temples. Writing on
wrappings can be used to date mummies.

ROMAN BOY

Inside these wrappings is the body
of a Roman boy. X-rays show that
he was about eight when he died.
He is lying with his hands by his
sides and is wearing a bracelet
on his right wrist.

TOOTSIES

Even the toenails on this
beautifully bandaged foot have
been individually wrapped.

A French archaeologist
discovers a mummy in the
ruins of Antinoe, 1896

Mummy masks

A BEAUTIFUL MASK did more than protect the mummy's face – it could also act as a substitute head if the mummy's real head was lost or damaged. When the dead person's spirit (the *Ba*, p. 12) returned to the tomb, it could recognize the mummy by its mask. One of the most famous works of art in the world is the stunning gold mask found on Tutankhamun's mummy (pp. 7, 39). The masks of pharaohs may all have been made of solid gold, often inlaid with beautiful gemstones. The use of gold was connected to the belief that the sun god, with whom the mummy hoped to be united, had flesh of pure gold. Less important mummies wore masks made from cartonnage, a sort of paper-mâché of linen or scrap papyrus gummed together with plaster or resin. The wet cartonnage was molded to fit the mummy. Once it had hardened, it could then be gilded (covered in gold leaf) or painted in rich colors.

Floral wrea

Gold earrir

Bead neckl

Winge scar beet

ALL DRESSED UP FOR THE AFTERLIFE
This Roman mummy mask shows a woman dressed in her best clothes and wearing her favorite jewelry. She is even wearing make-up so she will look her best for the gods.

Sacred flower

Bracelet

Gold headdress with wings of a vulture

Striped wig

FIT FOR A PRINCESS
This cartonnage mask from about 1900 B.C. belonged to a wealthy woman. She has not been identified, but the beautiful vulture headdress she is wearing suggests that she may have been a princess.

Raised relief coated in gold

GREEK GOLD
Cartonnage mummy masks were particularly popular by Greek and Roman times (pp. 42–43). This elegant gilded mask is rich in raised decoration, a typical feature of the period.

Prayer to Osiris to provide food

Prayer to Anubis for a good burial

Curly wig

Floral wreath

Pierced ears for wearing studs

WOODEN FEATURES
This mask was carved from wood and then painted. It comes from 1350 B.C. – the same period in which Tutankhamun was pharaoh (pp. 38–39).

SPITTING IMAGE
Ancient Egyptian masks were usually idealized, with perfect features and a calm and noble expression. Greek mummies (pp. 42–43) wore more personal masks with realistic features and vividly painted details. These masks seem to represent real people.

Collar of lotus petals

Linen strips holding mask and pectoral in place

Pectoral, a painted cartonnage chest decoration

TIED DOWN
After the careful embalming and wrapping processes, the mask was finally fitted over the mummy's head. It was then lashed in place with more bandages. Often a decorated pectoral (chest plate) and foot case (p. 27) were added in the same way.

Eye of Horus (wedjat)

Ba (soul) bird

EVERY PICTURE TELLS A STORY
This cartonnage mask from the Roman period is gilded and painted with many religious scenes. Glass eyes were added to create a more lifelike appearance.

Gods holding the Feather of Truth

19

Amulets and magic charms

ANCIENT EGYPTIANS WORE AMULETS, or charms, after they died, just as they did in life. They believed these charms had magical properties to protect the body from evil or bring good luck. Many different kinds of amulets, often representing plants, animals, or parts of the body, were placed inside a mummy's wrappings. Several hundred amulets have been found on a single mummy. They were positioned on the body according to the Book of the Dead (pp. 12–13), and many were inscribed with excerpts from these sacred writings. The particular stone or material used for the amulet was believed to give it extra power. Priests often spoke spells and prayers as the sacred amulets were placed on the mummy.

Clenched fist, to give power of action

Two finger amulet laid on embalming incision

THE THREE GRACES
Between them, the mother goddess Isis (right), her son Horus (center), and her sister Nephthy (left) gave powerful overa protection to the mumm

EYE OF HORUS
According to an ancient legend, the god Horus had his eye miraculously restored after he had lost it in a fight with evil. This eye symbol, known as the wedjat eye, became connected to healing. It was thought to protect the mummy's health and give the body new vitality.

Taweret

Bes

ODD COUPLE
The pregnant hippopotamus Taweret was the goddess of childbirth. Her lion-maned assistant, Bes, was a cheeky-looking dwarf who protected women and children.

FOUR SONS OF HORUS
These amulets guarded the vital organs, usually removed and placed in canopic jars (pp. 14–15). They are made from faience, a type of glazed pottery.

Imsety
(human head)

Duamutef
(jackal head)

Qebehsenuef
(falcon head)

Hapy
(baboon head)

HEAD WARMER
This bronze disc was tucked under a mummy's head. It carried a spell meant to keep the head warm.

Plaited wig

Real rings

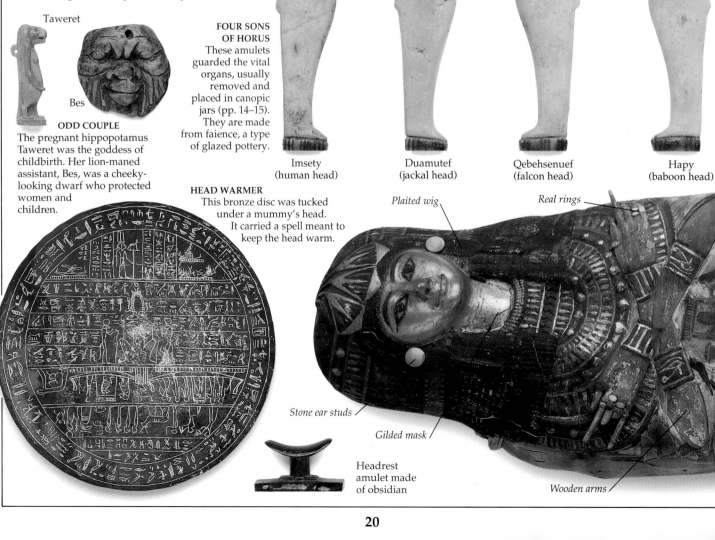

Stone ear studs

Gilded mask

Headrest amulet made of obsidian

Wooden arms

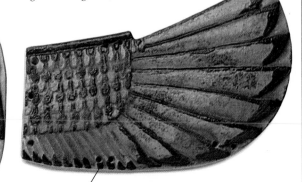

Scarab beetle

Holes for sewing into bandages

Beetle's wings, made of faience

WINGED HEART SCARAB
Egyptians thought that intelligence dwelled in the heart, not the brain. This heart amulet made sure that the mummy went into the afterlife with all of his or her wits intact.

Falcon head

STAIRWAY TO HEAVEN
These steps symbolize the stairs on Osiris' throne, which every mummy's spirit would have to climb (pp. 34-35).

Papyrus reed (p. 13)

Heart, made from a red-and-white stone called breccia

Heart scarab

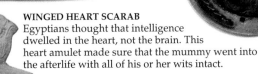

Scarab beetle

Girdle of Isis

CLOSE TO THE MUMMY'S HEART
This heart scarab has no wings. These important amulets were often set in a frame and sewn on top of the mummy's wrappings. The ancient Egyptians thought that the scarab beetle (p. 44) was born magically from a ball of dung. So it was not surprising that they associated it with rebirth after death. A spell from the Book of the Dead that would help in the Weighing of the Heart (p. 13) was written on the other side of the amulet.

GIRDLE OF ISIS
This knot amulet represents Isis, the mother goddess. It is made of red stone, to represent her blood. Placed on the chest, the girdle was a powerful symbol that protected the mummy.

Head of a lioness

Weight, made of blue faience

Shen, a circle of cord, a symbol of completeness and eternity

Plaque showing Anubis

Shabti figure

WELL PROTECTED
The upper part of the body usually received most of the amulets, with many grouped around the heart or just below the waist. This female mummy is protected by a fine selection of amulets – though most are still hidden among her bandages. She is also wearing some of her favorite jewelry.

Nut, the sky goddess, wrapping her wings around the mummy

Outer mummy
case base

Inner mummy
case base

Mummy cover
(top and bottom)

Outer mummy case lid

Inner mummy
case lid

Gilded
top half

Wedjat
eyes

Painted
wood

Wood completely
covered in gold

A MUMMY'S NEST
This nest of mummy cases was made for
Henutmehit, a priestess in the Egyptian capital of Thebes
around 1250 B.C. The fine gold decoration suggests that she was
very important. Her mummy, which has not been found, would have
been protected by the mummy cover. This has an upper and lower
part, both made of cartonnage. The mummy was then laid into two
wooden cases, with the inner case fitting inside the outer one. Both
have eyes and eyebrows made of a black volcanic glass called obsidian.

Mummy cases

AFTER AN ANCIENT EGYPTIAN HAD BEEN EMBALMED and bandaged, his or her body was placed in a coffin or mummy case. The case protected the mummy from wild animals and tomb thieves. More importantly, it was regarded as a substitute body and a house for the dead person's spirit. Mummy cases changed a lot through ancient Egypt's long history. The first ones were usually just plain rectangular wooden boxes. By the Middle Kingdom, about 2000 B.C., wealthy people were being placed inside two mummy cases for extra protection. Around the same time, the first mummiform (mummy-shaped) cases began to appear. By the New Kingdom, from 1550 to 1069 B.C., both inner and outer mummiform coffins were popular.

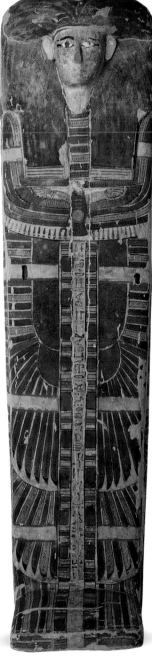

EARLY MUMMY CASE
About 5,000 years ago, an ancient Egyptian was placed in this reed basket and buried in the hot sand. Like a sand mummy (p. 8), he or she was laid in a hunched-up position with the knees tucked up by the face. But the basket stopped the sand from preserving the body, so only a skeleton remains.

FINISHING TOUCHES
This painting comes from the walls of the tomb of Ipuy, a sculptor during the reign of Ramesses the Great (pp. 36, 50). It shows workers putting the finishing touches on Ipuy's wooden mummy cases.

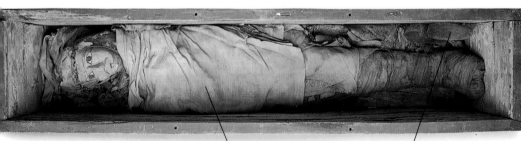

FACING THE RISING SUN
A masked man called Ankhef lies in his rectangular coffin from around 2020 B.C. At some point he must have been turned around, because he should be lying on his left side, with his head on the headrest, which is now by his feet. Mummies often faced east, so they could see the sun, a symbol of rebirth, rise over the desert each morning.

Body wrapped in shroud   *Headrest*   *False eyes*

WRAPPED IN FEATHERS
A vulture's feathers protect the owner of this mummy case lid. It is known as a *rishi* case, from the Arabic word for feathered.

PAINTED EYES
False eyes were painted on the east side of this wooden inner coffin (c. 2000 B.C.). Lying on its side, the mummy could "look out" through the eyes. Below them is a painted door, for the mummy's spirit to leave and reenter the coffin.

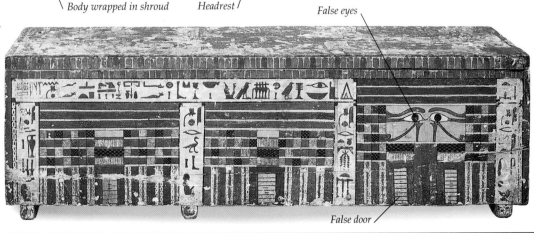

False door

23

Continued on next page

Outer coffin lid   Inner coffin   Masked mummy   Unwrapped mummy

TINY NEST FOR A TINY MUMMY
This is one of two tiny nests of coffins found among all the treasures in Tutankhamun's tomb (pp. 38–39). It contained the mummified body of an unborn child, probably the king's daughter. The wrapped mummy was wearing a mask and lying inside a gilded inner coffin. All this fit inside a second, outer coffin less than 19.5 inches (50 cm) long.

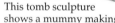

Sandaled feet

Wooden case of the priestess Katebet, c. 1300 B.C.

MUMMY CARGO
This tomb sculpture shows a mummy making the symbolic journey to Abydos, the city of the god Osiris (pp. 34–35).

Why cartonnage?
Wood was the ideal material for making mummy cases. But there are very few large trees in Egypt, and the best pieces of wood had to be imported. An excellent alternative was cartonnage (p. 18), which was cheap, light, and easy to shape and paint.

RED BRACES
The red braces on this inner case are a common feature of the period from 1000 to 800 B.C. They show that the owner was a priest or, as in this case, a priestess. The decorations in her hair are lotus blossoms (p. 30).

Red braces

SEX CHANGE
This coffin's pink face shows that it was made for a woman. But the inscription says the owner was a man, an official called Nesperennub, who lived around 800 B.C. Egyptians often took over other people's coffins in this way.

Napoleon's army (pp. 10–11) removed many mummy cases from their tombs and carried them back to France. Most are now in the Louvre Museum in Paris.

Detail from Léon Cogniet's paintings on the ceiling of the Campana room in the Louvre, show one of Napoleon's soldiers transporting a mummy case

MAGIC SYMBOLS
The symbols painted on cases were meant to protect the mummy or help it on the difficult voyage to the afterlife. Apart from gods and magic symbols, decoration included floral wreaths, elaborate wigs and collars, and jewelry. This is a selection of the most popular symbols.

Wig

Collar ending in falcon heads

Scarab beetle on sacred boat

Red braces

Sun

Winged god with ram's head

Winged Uraeus, the royal cobra

Sokar bird

One of four Sons of Horus

Wedjat eye or Eye of Horus

Nut, the sky goddess

Winged falcon, sacred to the god Horus

Djed pillar

Shen, symbol of eternity

Anubis, god of embalming

Apis bull carrying mummy

Mummy case decoration

There is nothing sad or depressing about Egyptian mummy cases, which are painted in bright and joyful colors. This is because the Egyptians were confident that the dead person had left for a better world. Skilled artists painted the surfaces with beautiful hieroglyphs and religious images. Scenes from the Book of the Dead (pp. 12–13) were common. Other scenes show the sun god, Re, whom the dead person was thought to join in heaven, or the scarab beetle, a symbol of rebirth (p. 44). The various gods associated with Osiris, in particular the four Sons of Horus (p. 20), were also painted on many coffins. Another popular figure was the sky goddess, Nut, who is often seen on the lid or floor of the coffin, with her feathery wings wrapped around the mummy in protection.

SIDE VIEW
Pasenhor was one of the many Libyans who settled in ancient Egypt. This is his outer coffin, made of very thick wood, from about 730 B.C.. The colorful decoration shows up beautifully against the white painted background.

MUMMY BOARD
Mummiform boards were sometimes put on top of the mummy. This board of a priestess from 950–900 B.C. is made of carved wood. This is covered by a layer of plaster painted in raised relief.

Continued on next page

Later mummy cases

By the Late Period of ancient Egyptian history, mummy case production was a thriving industry. Ready-made coffins could be bought off the rack in a range of sizes and styles. Usually an inner, cartonnage case was fitted inside one or two outer cases made of wood. The surface decorations became more and more complicated, and large gods and goddesses were painted on the insides. Designs and hieroglyphs naming and praising the owner were often added, to give each coffin a personal touch.

WHAT'S YOUR SIZE?
The largest outer cases are massive. Under three cases and layers of linen, the person was tiny in comparison.

BIG HEAD, BIG WIG
The outer coffin lid of Nesmin, from about 350 B.C. has a huge head. This is sunk into rounded shoulders carrying a big wig and collar

Mummy with Ba bird

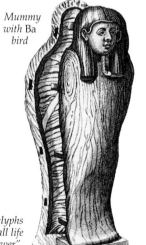

Hieroglyphs read "all life and power"

SURROUNDED BY GODS
A woman named Seshepenmehit was buried in these two wooden coffins around 650 B.C. The floor of her outer coffin is decorated with a figure of the god Ptah-Sokar-Osiris, a symbol of birth, death, and the afterlife. Both coffin lids are covered in columns of hieroglyphs and scenes from the Book of the Dead (pp. 12–13).

AND ON THE INSIDE...
One of the earliest European pictures of an Egyptian mummy, this engraving was published by a French consul to Egypt in 1735. It shows how the pegs in a wooden mummy case join the lid and base

Curved lid

Figures of Anubis

Corner posts

LACED FROM BEHIND
Wooden mummy cases came in two parts, the lid and the base. But inner cases made of cartonnage were normally made in one piece. This cartonnage case from c. 850 B.C. would have held the wrapped mummy of a young girl. The mummy must have been placed inside while the linen was damp and flexible. Once the case had dried, its back was laced up like a corset, with thongs that sealed the mummy in. Only then was the case painted.

FOUR-POSTER
Important officials who could not afford a sarcophagus might purchase an extra outer coffin. The priest Hor (c. 680 B.C.) had two mummiform cases, which lay inside a large rectangular box. Also made of wood, this third coffin has a curved lid held up by four corner posts. Every inch of the cases is covered with gods, hieroglyphs, and magic spells.

Cartonnage collar with falcon head at both ends

Apron, a painted body decoration

Face mask

Foot case

NOT MASKS
These faces were carved from wood and pegged onto mummy cases.

[R]EST IN PIECES
[T]he Ptolemaic period began in 304 B.C., [af]ter the conquest of Egypt by [A]lexander the Great in 332 B.C. The [in]ner cases of Ptolemaic mummies [co]nsisted of four pieces of cartonnage[—] [the] face mask, collar, apron, and foot [c]ase. These were placed directly onto [the] shroud and then held in place with [a] last layer of bandages.

[T]HE LATEST FASHION, A.D. 200
[I]n the Roman period, from 30 B.C. to [A].D. 395, coffins were painted with their [o]wners wearing daily clothes. This [R]oman woman left for the next world [in] a bright toga, worn with a stepped [w]ig and a lot of jewelry, including gold rings.

Ba bird

Hieroglyphs

SACRED BULL
The ancient Egyptians worshiped many animals (pp. 44–47). The sacred Apis Bull was the largest and most important. There was only one Apis at any one time. He was kept in great luxury beside the temple, where he was attended by servants and a harem of cows. This painting on a foot board shows the bull carrying a mummy to its tomb.

UNDER MY TOES
Gilded sandals like these were sometimes painted under a mummy's feet. The figures painted under the mummy's sandals are tiny enemies, symbolizing the dead person's victory over evil.

Colorful toga, a long piece of cloth wrapped around the body

Real rings stuck on fingers

Into the sarcophagus

A SARCOPHAGUS IS A COFFIN made of stone. The word means "flesh eater" in Greek, for the Greeks believed that a body laid inside would be dissolved by the stone. Sarcophagi were expensive, and only pharaohs, noblemen, or important officials were buried in them. They were also incredibly heavy, and had to be positioned in the tomb by gangs of workmen. During the funeral, the mummy was carried into the tomb and sealed in the sarcophagus. The first sarcophagi were plain rectangular boxes, but later ones were rounded to look like the mummies lying inside them.

HEAVY WEIGHT
This huge sarcophagus of basalt is nearly 9 ft (3 m) tall and weighs 5 tons. It belonged to Wahibra, an inspector of scribes.

DIGNIFIED IN DEATH
One of the most beautiful royal sarcophagi belongs to Seti I, a great warrior and the father of Ramesses II (pp. 36, 50–51). His tomb, found in 1817, is cut deep into a cliff in the Valley of the Kings (p. 10). The pharaoh's sarcophagus was in the burial chamber over 330 ft (100 m) below ground. It is made of calcite, a semitransparent stone. Seti I's mummy, found separately in the royal cache of 1881 (pp. 36–37), was remarkably well preserved.

VICEROY'S COFFIN
This is the inner sarcophagus of Merymose, the Viceroy of Nubia, c. 1380 B.C. It is one of the first stone coffins made for an important person who was *not* a pharaoh.

Feathered rishi decoration

Hieroglyphs, once inlaid with blue-green pigment

Fragment from lid of Seti I's sarcophagus, which shattered when lifted

Alexander
the Great

ROYAL BATHTUB
The last Egyptian pharaoh, Nactanebo II, was buried in this huge sarcophagus. It ended up in Alexandria, where the Greeks used it as a public bathtub. Before the hieroglyphics were translated, it was thought to have belonged to the Greek ruler Alexander the Great. Alexander's body has never been found, but ancient writings claim that he was preserved in a glass sarcophagus full of honey.

Drain holes added for use as bathtub

BACK AT REST
Tutankhamun (pp. 38–39) is the only pharaoh still lying in his tomb. His mummy has been returned to its outer gilded coffin and laid back in its huge sarcophagus. This stone coffin was originally housed inside four gilded shrines large enough to drive a car into. Behind it are wall paintings showing sacred funeral rituals.

PROFESSIONAL WEEPERS
Important Egyptians hired mourners for their funerals. These women would cry, wail, wave their arms, and throw dust in the air as the mummy was dragged into the tomb and laid in the sarcophagus.

Howard Carter (far right) watches Tutankhamun's outer mummy case is lifted out of the sarcophagus

WELL ARMED
This sarcophagus lid, made of red granite, covered the mummy of Setau, the Viceroy of Nubia. He was buried at Thebes around 1230 B.C. In his hands he holds two magical symbols, the girdle of Isis (p. 21) and the djed pillar (pp. 34–35).

HOUSE OF SPIRITS
Like the oldest mummy cases, early sarcophagi were regarded as palaces for the dead. This rectangular sarcophagus made of red granite comes from the Old Kingdom, around 2500 B.C. At either end are false doors, for the mummy's spirit to pass through when it leaves and reenters the coffin.

False door

Taking it with you

SLIPPERS, MAKEUP, A LOAF OF BREAD, a beautiful chair, some favorite earrings – the mummy had to be well prepared to enjoy life in the next world. Most of the artifacts that have survived from ancient Egypt were found in tombs, where they had been buried with the dead. Egypt's warm, dry climate has preserved many objects perfectly. Some mummies took the tools of their trade or symbols of their rank with them to the grave. Tutankhamun (pp. 38–39) was found with his childhood toys. Glamorous women were buried with their wigs, combs, fans, and mirrors. Musicians took along their instruments, and some people were even laid to rest with a board game, to while away the days of leisure in the afterlife.

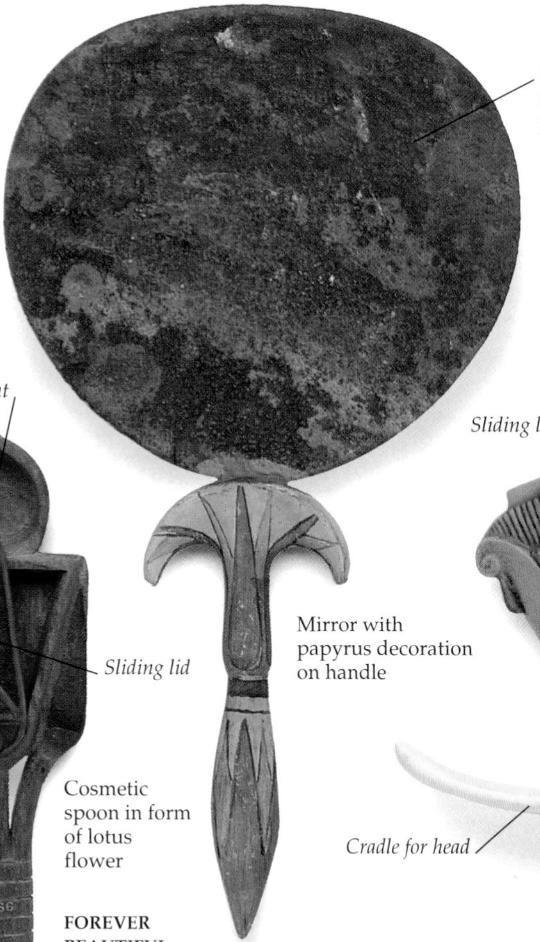

Corroded bronze surface, once polished for reflection

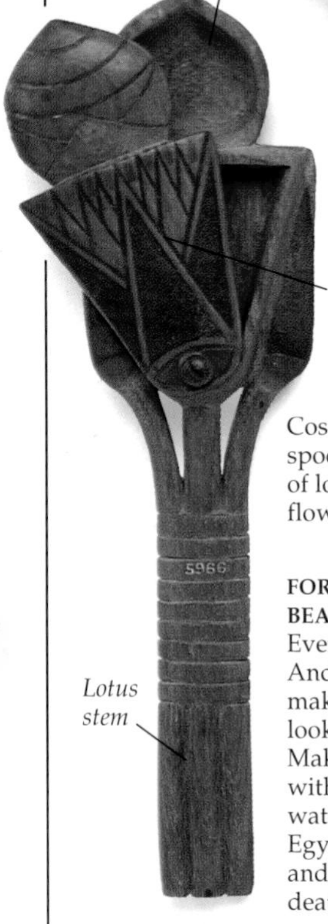

Make-up compartment

Sliding lid

Sliding lid

EARTHLY COMFORTS
Sandals were a luxury, as most Egyptians went around barefoot. This padded leather pair is unusual. Most sandals were made from reeds found on the banks of the Nile.

Mirror with papyrus decoration on handle

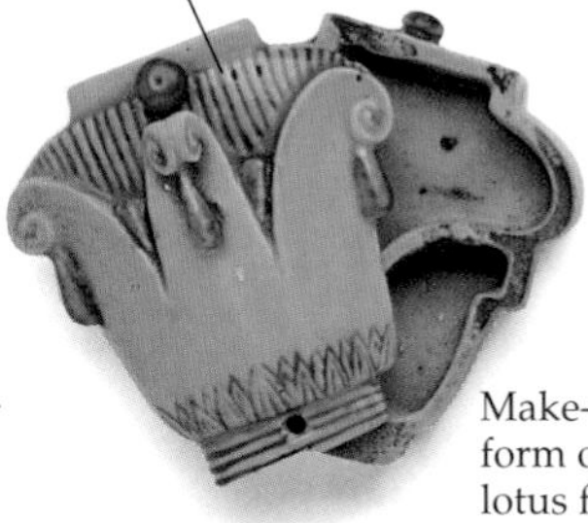

Sliding lid

Make-up box in form of stylized lotus flower

Cosmetic spoon in form of lotus flower

Cradle for head

Lotus stem

FOREVER BEAUTIFUL
Every mummy wanted to look good for the gods. Ancient Egyptian men, women, and children all wore make-up, particularly *kohl*, a type of eye-paint. *Kohl* looked good and protected against eye infections. Make-up was usually kept in containers decorated with lotus flowers and buds. The lotus, a type of water-lily, was a sacred plant. The Egyptians saw its daily opening and closing as a symbol of life, death, and rebirth.

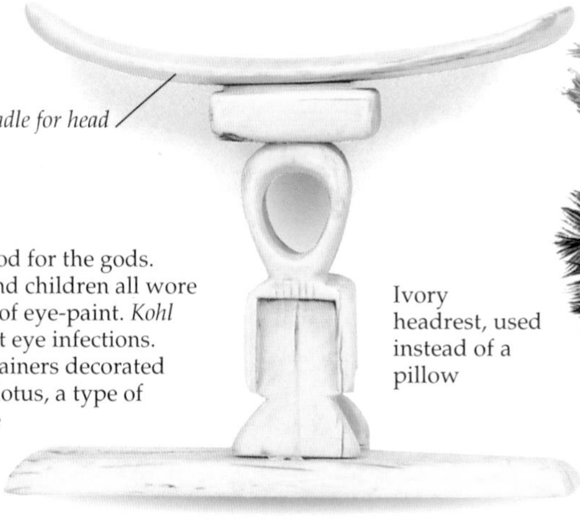

Ivory headrest, used instead of a pillow

STAY COOL
In the hot climate, fans were a sign of wealth and sophistication. Pharaohs and other nobles even had special servants just to fan them.

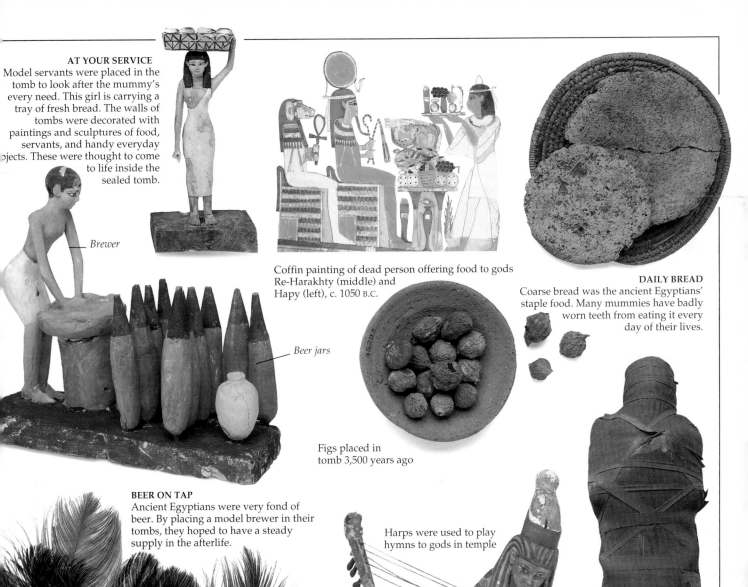

AT YOUR SERVICE
Model servants were placed in the tomb to look after the mummy's every need. This girl is carrying a tray of fresh bread. The walls of tombs were decorated with paintings and sculptures of food, servants, and handy everyday objects. These were thought to come to life inside the sealed tomb.

Brewer

Coffin painting of dead person offering food to gods Re-Harakhty (middle) and Hapy (left), c. 1050 B.C.

DAILY BREAD
Coarse bread was the ancient Egyptians' staple food. Many mummies have badly worn teeth from eating it every day of their lives.

Beer jars

Figs placed in tomb 3,500 years ago

BEER ON TAP
Ancient Egyptians were very fond of beer. By placing a model brewer in their tombs, they hoped to have a steady supply in the afterlife.

Harps were used to play hymns to gods in temple

Pair of bronze cymbals

Drawer for holding the pieces

Ivory Senet board

Blue faience game pieces

THE GAME OF LIFE
Senet was ancient Egypt's most popular board game. Senet boards were placed in the tomb to symbolize the dead person's contest with evil to gain eternal life.

ENDLESS JAM
This mummy may have been a professional musician who took his trusty cymbals with him to play in the next world.

Ivory feather holder

Wood handle

Ostrich feathers, added according to paintings of fans found on tomb walls

Workers for the afterlife

THE ANCIENT EGYPTIANS were an agricultural people, and every year they were all required to do some farming and irrigation work for the government. But rich Egyptians could avoid this work by paying someone to do it for them. When the mummy got to the Field of Reeds, as the Egyptians called heaven, he or she would have to do similar work, sowing and reaping for the god Osiris (pp. 34–35). So from early on, wealthy people were buried with shabtis (worker figures) to do their work after death. Shabtis were inscribed with Chapter Six of the Book of the Dead, which promised "O shabti, if the deceased is called upon to do any of the work required there…you shall say 'Here I am, I will do it.'" In the early New Kingdom (about 1500 B.C.), a single shabti seemed to be enough to guarantee an easy afterlife. But by 1000 B.C., rich Egyptians were being buried with 401 shabtis, one for every day of the year, plus 36 bosses, armed with whips to keep the workers from slacking as they sweated in the heavenly fields.

Overseer or boss shabti wearing skirt and carrying whip

EARLY DIGGE
Before the custom
shabtis, painted woode
servants and workers wer
placed in tombs. Unlik
shabtis, this worker
not shaped lik
a mumm

BOX OF WORKERS
Shabti figures were often packed up in beautifully painted wooden boxes. This shabti box belonged to the priestess Henutmehit, whose golden coffins are on page 22.

Dead priestess gives offerings of food to gods

Gilded collar

WOMEN WORKERS
These wooden shabti figures were both made for women from the 18th Dynasty, about 1560 to 1320 B.C.

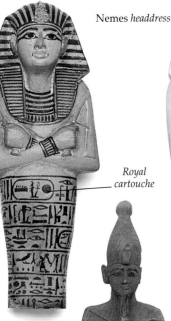

Nemes *headddress*

Royal cartouche

Shabti of Pharaoh Seti I

Cartouche: oval-shaped inscription with king's name written in hieroglyphs

Shabti of Pharaoh Amenhotep III

Shabti of Pharaoh Amosis

ROYAL SHABTIS
The earliest surviving royal shabti (above) belonged to Amosis, a pharaoh who died in c. 1546. It is wearing a *Nemes* headdress made from cloth folded over the hair. Other royal shabtis, like this one of Amenhotep III (left), wear the domed crown of Upper Egypt.

ALL SORTS
Stone, wood, clay, wax, bronze – shabtis were made of all kinds of materials. But the most common was faience, a type of earthenware heated up with quartz to make it look like tin.

MODEL COFFINS
Shabtis were sometimes put in elaborate cases made to look like real mummy cases. This one is made of blue faience.

WELL EQUIPPED
Many shabtis carry hoes, picks, seed baskets, and other tools. These tell us a lot about farming in ancient Egypt.

Pick

Hoe

Lid of inner wooden case on right

Stone shabti in wooden mummy case and square outer coffin

33

The mummy and the god Osiris

Atef *crown*

Crook

THE GOD OSIRIS was said to have triumphed over death, and every ancient Egyptian wanted to follow his example. Legend told that far back in history, Osiris was a good pharaoh who was murdered by his evil brother, Seth. But his wife, Isis, and son, Horus, brought Osiris back to life. The story of the dead king's miraculous resurrection gave Egyptians hope in everlasting life. So to be reborn, a dead person tried to be identified with Osiris in every possible way. Mummies were prepared in exactly the same way as the body of Osiris had been long ago. If all went well, the mummy would "become an Osiris" and live forever.

Brightly colored coffin painting of Osiris wearing cobra crown and protected by falcons

Flail

Atef *crown made of two ostrich feathers*

Painted wooden statue of Osiris with green face and *atef* crook

Crook

Flail

TOOLS OF THE TRADE
These two statues of Osiris would have been placed in tombs or temples. They both show Osiris wearing an *atef*, a tall, feathered crown. In his hands the dead pharaoh is holding a crook and a flail. From the earliest times, the Egyptians associated these agricultural tools with kingship and justice. Osiris carried them when he sat and judged dead people's souls in the afterlife (p. 13).

KEEP A STRAIGHT BACK
The djed pillar is an amulet placed in the wrappings of a mummy (pp. 20–21). It was believed to represent the backbone of Osiris, and was thought to give the mummy strength after death.

MUMMY AND SON
The goddess Isis was the wife of Osiris. In this statue she is holding their son, Horus. The ancient Egyptians respected her as a devoted wife and loving mother.

Bronze statue of Osiris wearing *atef* crown

FLAIL
A wooden flail from a statue of Osiris. Like the scepters carried by European kings and queens, the flail was a symbol of power and authority.

GREEN FACE
Among other things, the all-important Osiris was the god of vegetation and natural rebirth. In this role he was connected to the yearly flood of the Nile, which kept Egypt's lands green and fertile. Mummy cases often have green faces to link them with this aspect of Osiris.

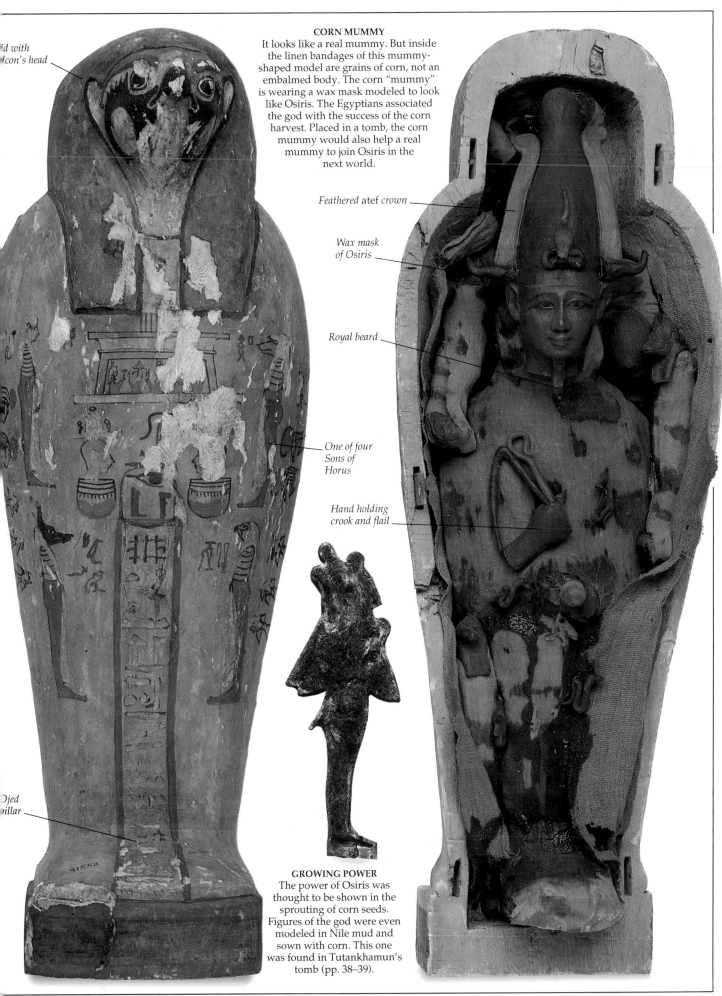

...d with
...con's head

...Djed
...illar

CORN MUMMY
It looks like a real mummy. But inside the linen bandages of this mummy-shaped model are grains of corn, not an embalmed body. The corn "mummy" is wearing a wax mask modeled to look like Osiris. The Egyptians associated the god with the success of the corn harvest. Placed in a tomb, the corn mummy would also help a real mummy to join Osiris in the next world.

Feathered atef *crown*

Wax mask
of Osiris

Royal beard

One of four
Sons of
Horus

Hand holding
crook and flail

GROWING POWER
The power of Osiris was thought to be shown in the sprouting of corn seeds. Figures of the god were even modeled in Nile mud and sown with corn. This one was found in Tutankhamun's tomb (pp. 38–39).

41553

The royal mummies

THE FAMOUS PHARAOHS of the New Kingdom were buried at Thebes, in a desolate valley called the Valley of the Kings (p. 10). The tombs were cut deep into the rock. But despite all the precautions, they were robbed again and again in ancient times. Each time the priests had to rewrap the mummies and bury them again. Around 1000 B.C., they decided to group the royal mummies together and hide them in two caches (secret hiding places). The dead pharaohs lay hidden in these caches for nearly 3,000 years. The first cache was found in the early 1870s by three brothers who lived nearby. They kept it a secret and began to sell the treasures bit by bit. But the priceless antiquities were eventually traced to them, and in 1881 archaeologists entered a tomb near Deir el-Bahari. They were amazed to find 40 mummies, among them famous pharaohs such as Seti I and Ramesses II. The second cache, found in 1898, held another 16 mummies, ten of them royal. When this cache was shipped to Cairo, the customs officers at the city's gate had no idea how to classify it. In the end they decided to tax the dead pharaohs at the same rate as dried fish!

INSIDE THE PYRAMIDS
The mummies of the kings who built the Giza pyramids have not survived. Despite their hidden entrances sealed with huge blocks of stone, these tombs were looted in ancient times. Once inside, robbers had to find the burial chamber in the darkness, along narrow passages full of false corridors and traps.

LABELING THE KIN
To avoid confusion, priests wrote the pharao names on the outer shrou This mummy is inscribed w the name Ramses

RAMSES THE GREAT
The famous Ramses II ruled for 67 years, from 1279 to 1212 B.C. He had a reputation as a great warrior, which he seems to have greatly exaggerated. He and his many wives had over 100 children, and he was probably in his nineties when he died. Ancient Egyptians were short by modern standards, around 5 ft 3 in (1.60 m) on average. But Ramses II's mummy, found in the 1881 cache, is 6 ft (1.83 m) tall (p. 50).

REPAIR JOB
The mummy of King Siptah, who died in 1188 B.C., was badly damaged by tomb robbers searching for precious amulets in his bandages. The priests who moved him around 1000 B.C. put his broken arm in a splint before rewrapping him.

Wrapped mummy of King Siptah as it was found in 1881

Unwrapped mummy of King Siptah

GASTON MASPERO
This French archaeologist (third from right) supervised the unwrapping of the royal mummies in Cairo. "And when I see, and touch, the bodies of so many illustrious persons we never imagined could be more than names to us," he wrote later, "I … find it hard to believe that I am not dreaming."

MISTAKEN IDENTITY

This well-preserved mummy was found wrapped in a shroud inscribed with the name of Tuthmosis I. But examination of the mummy suggests that it is someone else. Surviving historical records show that this pharaoh lived to about 50 years of age. But the mummy is in excellent health and seems to belong to a much younger man. The mummy's true identity is still a mystery.

Nemes headcloth, *a sign of royalty*

Wood covered in plaster

Remaining fragments of gold leaf

TUTHMOSIS I
A painting in a temple in Thebes shows the real king Tuthmosis I. This accurate copy was made by Howard Carter.

GARLANDS OF FLOWERS
Flower wreaths were placed around a mummy's neck as it was laid in the coffin. When the lid of Amenhotep I's coffin was lifted, the sweet smell of flowers filled the room, 3,000 years after his burial. A wasp that had been attracted by the smell had been trapped in the coffin all those years ago. Its mummified body was found next to the king's.

Ear of corn found in coffin

Fragments of wreaths placed on mummy

UNKNOWN QUEEN
Egyptologists are still not sure about the identity of this elderly woman with wonderful hair. Her mummy was found in the second royal cache of 1898. Some experts believe she is Hatshepsut, a female pharaoh who is often shown wearing the royal false beard. Others think she is Queen Tiy, one of the wives of Amenhotep III. Tiy is probably the grandmother of Tutankhamun (pp. 38–39).

ROYAL COFFIN
The mummy case of King Intef (c. 1650 B.C.) is made from a hollowed-out tree trunk. This was plastered and covered with gold leaf engraved with a *rishi* feather design (p. 23). Robbers often stripped the gold leaf off royal coffins like this.

A KING AT REST
The second cache of royal mummies was found in the tomb of Amenhotep II in 1898. Most of the mummies were shipped to Cairo, but Amenhotep was left lying in his sarcophagus where he had been found. Shortly after this photo was taken, a band of robbers overcame the armed guards and ripped open his bandages, looking for valuable amulets.

CRUEL DEATH
The strangest body found among the royal mummies was this unknown man. His face is distorted with agony, and his mouth is open as if he was screaming. He must have died horribly, perhaps by being poisoned, suffocated, or even buried alive. His body was wrapped in a sheepskin, a material the Egyptians thought was unclean. No one knows what horrible crime he committed to deserve such a cruel death.

The treasures of Tutankhamun

Howard Carter (center) and his team stare in wonder at the sarcophagus through a door in the fourth shrine

ON NOVEMBER 26, 1922, Howard Carter peered through a small hole into a dark tomb in the Valley of the Kings (pp. 10, 36–37). "As my eyes grew accustomed to the light," he wrote later, "… I was struck dumb with amazement." The English archaeologist and his wealthy supporter Lord Carnarvon had just discovered the tomb of the pharaoh Tutankhamun, sealed over 3,200 years before. Five years of methodical exploration had led them to the only fully intact royal tomb ever found – and probably the most exciting archaeological discovery ever made. Inside was the king's mummy, wearing a superbly crafted mask of solid gold. The body lay in a nest of three gold mummy cases, each fitting inside the next. The cases rested in turn in a sarcophagus surrounded by four gilded wooden shrines and an amazing array of statues, furniture, and jewelry. As Carter put it, it was a room full of "gold – everywhere the glint of gold."

KING AND QUEEN
The carving on this ebony and ivory box shows Tutankhamun in a garden receiving flowers from his queen. When his father, the powerful pharaoh Akhenaten, died, Tutankhamun was no more than nine years old. He probably never had much real power, and would barely be remembered if his tomb had not survived in such perfect condition.

SCARAB PENDANT
This pendant of a winged scarab beetle is made of gold and semi-precious stones. The design spells out the three hieroglyphs – Neb, Kheperu, and Re – of Tutankhamun's name.

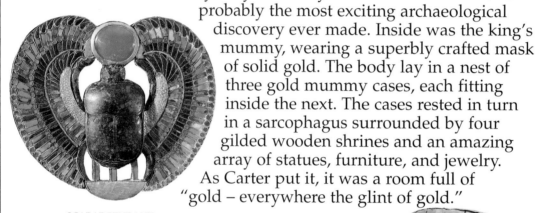

Gold sheets covering wood frame

Small shrine made to hold a sacred statue

Decorated panels

Silver door bolts

Sled runners so shrine could be dragged into tomb

THE KING'S DUMMY
This painted wooden "dummy" shows the king as he must have looked when he died c. 1324 B.C. It was probably dressed in his clothes and jewelry.

Shaved head

Bead vest

THE MUMMY
The king's mummy was poorly preserved because of chemical reactions with embalming resins. He was slightly built and stood about 5 ft 5 in (1.65 m) tall. Studies of his teeth gave an age of 16 or 17, though he may have been as old as 22. X-rays showed damage to his skull, but his actual cause of death is uncertain. The uneasy political situation during his reign suggests that he may have been murdered.

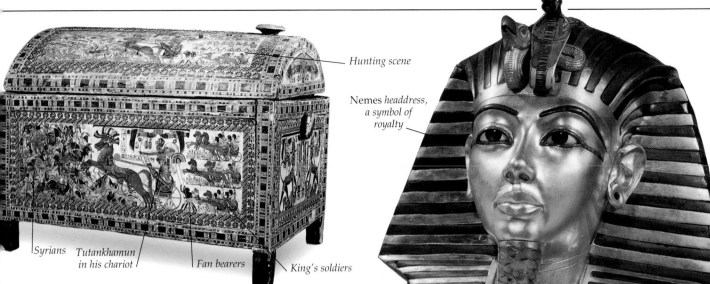

Hunting scene

Syrians

Tutankhamun in his chariot

Fan bearers

King's soldiers

Nemes *headdress, a symbol of royalty*

Falcon-headed collar

PAINTED BOX

This wooden box was stuffed with clothes, including the pharaoh's sandals. It is painted with scenes from Tutankhamun's life. On this side, he can be seen leading his army to victory over the Syrians. But it is unlikely that the king ever went to war, and the painting is thought to be a symbolic representation of the pharaoh's supreme power. In two similar scenes on the lid, the young king hunts lions, ostriches, and antelopes in the desert.

SLOW GOING

An Italian newspaper from 1924 tells the tale of the amazing discovery. Though Carter and Carnavon found the tomb in November 1922, Carter was so careful and painstaking in his work that he didn't begin to open the coffins until October 1925. It took him almost a decade to examine the entire contents of the tomb.

Inlaid lapis lazuli, a blue stone

GOLD MASK

The king's mummy mask was made of solid gold inlaid with colorful glass and stones, including dark blue lapis lazuli. It weighed over 22.5 lb (10.2 kg). The pharaoh is wearing a *nemes* headdress (p. 33), and a vulture and a cobra sit on his brow.

A NEST OF GOLD AND GEMSTONES

This is Tutankhamun's middle mummy case. Like the outer case, it was made of wood covered in gold and colored stones. It fitted so snugly inside the outer case that Carter had a lot of difficulty lifting it out. Inside it was a third, inner case. This was solid gold and weighed an unbelievable 245 lb (110.4 kg).

Inlaid pieces of red, blue, and turquoise glass

Feathered *rishi* design

Curse of the mummy

"DEATH SHALL COME ON SWIFT WINGS to him that toucheth the tomb of pharaoh." In the spring of 1923, newspapers around the world claimed that this dramatic inscription had been found inside Tutankhamun's tomb (pp. 38–39). The excitement was caused by the sudden death of Lord Carnarvon, one of the first to enter the tomb. Many people claimed that the dead pharaoh was angry and had "cursed" all those who had disturbed his rest. The curse has since been blamed for the deaths of many people connected with the discovery. Some now believe that the deaths may have been caused by bacteria or even atomic radiation sealed inside the tomb. But the deaths can all be explained, and the famous inscription never existed. Howard Carter and most of the others who entered the tomb lived on for many years. The most important wish of a pharaoh was that his name should live forever. Considering how famous Tutankhamun has become since his tomb was found, he should be pleased, not angry.

MUMMY POWDER
Ground-up mummy was believed to have magical powers. It was used as an occult potion and was a popular medicine in the 16th and 17th centuries. Powdered mummy was also used to make brown pigment for artists. The paint was called *Caput Mortuum*, Latin for "dead head."

FIRST VICTIM
Lord Carnarvon, Howard Carter's sponsor, had first come to Egypt because of his poor health. Early in 1923, he was bitten by a mosquito, and the bite became infected after he reopened it while shaving. A fever developed, and he died on April 5, 1923, just over four months after he and Carter had entered Tutankhamun's tomb. It was later said that the lights of Cairo went out at the moment of his death. Another story associated with the curse was that Carter's canary had been swallowed by a cobra on the day the tomb was opened. Tutankhamun's famous mummy mask has a cobra on the brow.

Lord Carnarvon's death certificate

Lord Carnarvon's cutthroat razor

Real mummy of Ramses III

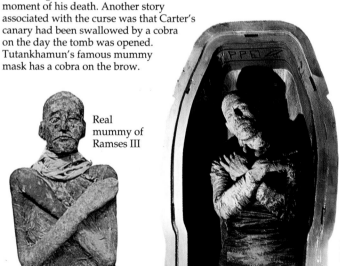

Boris Karloff in *The Mummy*

DANGEROUS SPELLS
This is one of four "magic bricks" that were found in the tomb of the priestess Henutmehit (pp. 22, 32). The bricks were placed at the four corners of the tomb and were believed to have supernatural powers. A spell from the Book of the Dead was inscribed on the mud surface of each brick. One of them reads "You who come to trap (steal), I will not let you trap … I am the protection for the Osiris Henutmehit." This was meant to keep away any intruders who might disturb the priestess' mummy in her tomb.

Wooden figure attached to magic brick

Inscription in hieratic, a script that developed from hieroglyphics

Clay brick

THE MUMMY BECOMES A FILM STAR
The angry mummy disturbed from the sleep of centuries proved a great subject for horror films. The first was *The Mummy*, from 1932, which starred Boris Karloff as the mummified priest Imhotep (above). His appearance was based on the real mummy of the pharaoh Ramses III (left), found in the 1881 royal cache (pp. 36–37). In the film, Imhotep is brought back to life by a magic spell read aloud by an archaeologist.

FEAR WILL FREEZE YOU WHEN YOU FACE...

"THE MUMMY"

ALL NEW!
IN TERRIFYING TECHNICOLOR!

THE MUMMY'S REVENGE
Alongside *Dracula* and *Frankenstein*, the mummy bent on revenge became one of the most popular monsters in Hollywood horror films. This is a poster for a 1959 remake of *The Mummy*, made in color and starring Christopher Lee. The many other films included *The Mummy's Hand*, *The Mummy's Shroud*, *The Mummy's Curse*, *Blood from the Mummy's Tomb* – even *Abbott and Costello Meet the Mummy*.

The archaeologist's assistant in *Raiders of the Lost Ark* finds herself face to face with a tomb full of mummies

LOST IN THE TOMB
A newspaper story from 1934 tells of a Hungarian tourist who was lost in the tomb of Ramses II during a visit to the Valley of the Kings. She was found the next day, lying speechless at the foot of a statue of the pharaoh. Passing a night in the cold, pitch-black tomb had completely terrified her.

SILENT SHRIEK
Many mummy heads were collected in the 19th century and displayed as curiosities in European homes. Travelers to Egypt could buy them from dealers as part of a busy souvenir trade. This gruesome head was mounted under a glass dome. Nobody knows where it comes from, whom it belonged to, or how old it is. Its grizzly features inspired some of the mummies used as props in the popular 1981 film *Raiders of the Lost Ark*. These were made of silicon rubber.

Greek and Roman mummies

MANY GREEKS HAD SETTLED IN EGYPT long before it was invaded by Alexander the Great (p. 29) in 332 B.C. Like the Romans who arrived in 30 B.C., the Greeks adopted the Egyptian custom of mummification. They took great care in wrapping their dead in elaborate geometric patterns. But beneath the linen, Greek and Roman mummies are usually badly embalmed. The mummies were laid to rest in open ground, not tombs, and several generations were often buried together in family graves. Some of the most interesting mummies from the Roman period were discovered in a cemetery in the Faiyum region of Egypt. Instead of having idealized faces like the ones found on Egyptian masks, they wear a realistic picture of the dead person. This sometimes takes the form of a plaster mask. But more often, portraits were painted on a wooden panel or straight onto the shroud.

ROMAN CAT
The ancient Greeks and Romans made mummies of all kinds of animals (pp. 44–47). This preserved cat is wearing a painted plaster mask. Two colors of linen bandages have been wrapped in an intricate "window" pattern.

THE LIVING DEAD
These mummy portraits are painted on wooden panels in colored wax. They may have been done while the person was alive and hung in the home until he or she died. The hairstyles, jewelry, and clothing tell us a lot about everyday life in Roman-occupied Egypt around the time of Christ.

Gilded studs

FOREVER YOUNG
X-rays of this mummy of a Roman boy showed that he was in his early teens when he died. The elaborate bandages are decorated with gilded studs.

PLASTER MASK
Some Greek mummies wore plaster masks that made them look like they were sitting up in the coffin. Many of these masks are covered in gold and have inset eyes of stone or glass to make them look more realistic.

Painted foot case

GOLDEN GIRL

This Roman girl died in Egypt at the age of eight or nine. She was not properly embalmed, but her skin was coated in a dark, liquid resin to make it tough and waterproof. Her body was then covered in thin pieces of beaten gold. These were meant to connect her to the sun god, who was thought to have flesh of gold.

Gold eye covers

Gold tongue cover

Gold nipple covers

Inscription in Greek

Figure of Osiris

MUMMY I.D.

Mixing up the bodies in the embalming tent could have been disastrous. To avoid confusion, Roman embalmers tied a wooden label around each mummy's neck. Mummy labels are often inscribed with the dead person's name, his or her age, profession, parents, even the date of death or where the mummy was to be buried. Some labels also carry a prayer for the dead person's soul, which relatives had bought instead of a tombstone.

GOLD LEAVES

The Romans placed pieces of gold over a mummy's sensitive parts. The tongue plate was probably meant to allow the mummy to speak.

Side view of Roman girl's head, showing eyelashes and gold leaf on face

Pieces of gold leaf

ROYAL BIRD

The falcon soared to great heights in the skies of ancient Egypt. So it is not surprising that it became associated with the sky god, Horus, who came to life as the pharaoh. In Greek and Roman times, falcons were mummified by the thousands and buried in special cemeteries with other sacred animals (pp. 44–47).

DEATH OF CLEOPATRA

Cleopatra, the last Greek ruler of Egypt, died in 30 B.C. Roman historians said that she committed suicide by holding a poisonous snake to her breast. Though there is no evidence to support the story, it has been painted and retold many times. Cleopatra's body was probably mummified and buried with all the ceremony due to an Egyptian queen. She was supposedly buried lying next to her lover, Mark Antony, but their tomb has never been found.

Animal mummies

THE ANCIENT EGYPTIANS MUMMIFIED many animals with the same care they took for people. Favorite pets were occasionally mummified and put in the tomb with their owners to keep them company in the afterlife. But most animals were embalmed for religious reasons. Animals were thought to be representatives or spiritual messengers of the gods. Many gods became naturally associated with one or more animals that shared the same qualities. The cow, for instance, which took such tender care of its young, was associated with Hathor, the goddess of love and motherhood. Special places became the centers of worship for major gods and goddesses. Here the animals sacred to these gods were mummified and buried in enormous cemeteries. By the later period of ancient Egyptian history, a huge religious industry flourished and millions of animals were bred just to be mummified.

Mummy of a wild dog or jackal, sacred to Anubis, the god of embalming (pp. 10, 13–15).

SACRED BULL
When he died, the sacred Apis Bull (p. 27) was embalmed with the same care and ceremony shown to a pharaoh.

Bronze case for the mummy of a shrew mouse, sacred animal of the god Horus (p. 20)

ROYAL SERPENT
Bronze container for the mummy of an eel or cobra. The snake's beard and crown show its association with royalty.

TWINS
These two falcons were embalmed and mummified together, to strengthen their magical association with the god Horus (p. 20).

A limestone case for a mummified scarab beetle, the smallest creature to be embalmed

ROLLING ACROSS THE SKY
The scarab beetle rolls up balls of dung and pushes them around. The Egyptians believed the beetle god Khepri rolled the sun across the sky in the same way.

Unwrapped mummy of a crocodile

Reeds used to pad out crocodile shape

Linen bandages

ON THE MENU?
An unwrapped mummified fish. Fish were sacred in some parts of Egypt, where they were never caught or eaten. In other areas, they were on the menu. This often led to violent conflicts between neighboring towns.

IN THE NILE, CROCODILE
In ancient times, the Nile River was full of crocodiles, which were feared for their ferocity. They were sacred to Sobek, a god of the water. Tame crocs were kept in luxury, fed on fine meats and wine and dressed in gold jewelry. The largest mummified crocodile ever found was 15 ft (4.6 m) long.

Painted plaster
mask for a
falcon mummy

Head of a
mummified goose,
sacred to the god
Amun

SACRED IBIS

Three kinds of ibis were
found in ancient Egypt. The
migrant species with brown
plumage still visits the country
every year. But the bronze-
colored crested ibis and the
beautiful sacred ibis (right) are
now extinct there.

*Head and
neck made
of bronze*

SCRIBE GOD

This gold
container holds
the mummified
body of an ibis.
Four million
embalmed ibises were
discovered at a single
animal cemetery, each in its
individual pot. They would have
been dedicated to Thoth, the god
of scribes and writing. Thoth was
usually depicted with a human
body and the head of an ibis.

ROOST
IN PEACE

The mummy of a falcon lies in
this coffin made of cartonnage
(p. 18). The lid is richly painted
with a floral collar and a winged
scarab beetle. The designs are
just like the ones on human
mummy cases.

Feet made of bronze

*Wooden body
covered in gold leaf*

Prominent teeth

*Geometric wrapping common
in Roman period*

*Eyes, which bulge on
top of crocodile's head*

Continued on next page

The sacred cat

The graceful, green-eyed cats that leaped and purred around ancient Egyptian homes were a lot like the pets we keep today. Ancient Egyptian records show that cats were kept as pets as early as 2100 B.C. By the late period of ancient Egyptian history, the cat was a sacred animal. Writing about 450 B.C., the Greek historian Herodotus (p. 14) described how carefully cats were protected. Anyone who killed a cat could be punished by death. When a cat died, some families even took their beloved pet's body to the city of Bubastis, the center of worship for the cat goddess Bastet. Here the dead pet was embalmed, wrapped, and laid in a special cat-shaped coffin before being buried in a cat cemetery.

CAT WRAP
To mummify a cat, the embalmers began by removing its insides. Then they filled the pet's body cavity with earth or sand and wrapped it in bandages that had been soaked in natron (pp. 14-15) or treated with resin. This fine mummy is wrapped in an elaborate diamond pattern.

Green hea[d] symboliz[es] bronze mas[k] worn b[y] mumm[y]

White body represents linen wrappings of mummy inside case

Mummified cat

Cat mummy with comical face

TIGHT FIT
To produce a compact mummy, the embalmers laid the cat's front legs by its side and tucked its back legs up against its belly. The cat's tail was then curled up between its feet.

*Pierced ear, which
probably once held a
gold earring*

BRONZE BASTET
The yearly festival
celebrating the cat
goddess Bastet was
one of the most
important events on
the ancient Egyptian
calendar. This statue
of Bastet made from
bronze has inlaid eyes
of colored glass. Many
of these elegant figures
wore gold rings in their ears
and noses. Thousands of
images of Bastet were set up
in temples by priests, so
worshippers could place
offerings of food and milk
before them. The priests also
bred many cats specially for
mummification.

Bronze container made to hold the
mummified paw of a cat

THE BALD TRUTH
Shaving was seen as a way of cleansing the
spirit, and ancient Egyptian priests and
priestesses all shaved their heads. When a
pet cat died, a whole household might go
into mourning and shave their eyebrows
as a mark of respect.

*Wooden case with
door at back*

PURR-SONALIZED COFFINS
These wooden cat coffins were all found
at Bubastis, the biggest center of cat
worship. Each one contained the well-
wrapped mummy of a cat. The largest
one shows an idealized, graceful cat, but
the other two are more natural and
humorous. In the 19th century, some
300,000 Egyptian cat mummies were
shipped to Liverpool in England, where
they were turned into fertilizer and sold
by the ton.

Unwrapping the mummy's secrets

THE SCIENTIFIC STUDY OF MUMMIES does more than reveal how the ancient Egyptians embalmed their dead. Autopsies of ancient bodies can also show how people lived, what they ate, and what diseases they suffered from. In the 19th century, many mummies were unwrapped by surgeons. But their findings were limited by the technology of the age. Nowadays, ruining the careful bandaging and dissecting the body is considered destructive and disrespectful. The invention of X-ray analysis in 1895 meant that mummies could be electronically "unwrapped" without being damaged. Early equipment was heavy and awkward. But by the 1960s, powerful, mobile X-ray units that could be brought into museums had been developed. The latest scanning equipment can "see" through the bandages and create complex, three-dimensional images of the body within. A small tissue sample from the mummy can be rehydrated (wetted) and its cell structure studied. Even DNA, a person's basic genetic structure, can be identified. Some scientists believe that genetic analysis may one day help find a cure for modern viruses.

CAIRO AUTOPSY
Daniel Fouquet, a French doctor, unwraps the mummy of Tawedjatra, a priestess who died around 1000 B.C. This historic autopsy took place at the Cairo Museum in 1891. It was attended by the leading French Egyptologists of the day, along with several society women.

ESTIMATING AGE
This mummy of a man is lying in a coffin made c. 1000 B.C. for Tawuhenut, a female singer. Studies of the man's teeth and bones put his age at 20 to 35. More accurate estimates can be made for mummies who died before the age of 25 when their teeth and bones were still growing.

UNDER THE MICROSCOPE
In 1908, Dr. Margaret Murray (second from right) and her colleagues unwrapped and dissected a mummy at Manchester University in England. They kept some tissue samples. These were examined in the 1970s as part of a major mummy survey led by Dr. Rosalie David. When rehydrated and viewed under a microscope, the tissues revealed evidence of a lung disease called silicosis. Desert sandstorms and the dusty climate may have caused breathing problems like silicosis for many ancient Egyptians.

Artificial eyes

Scarab beetle amulet with wings wrapping around neck

Dense mass may be a pot

ALL IS REVEALED
This is a xeroradiograph of a mummy wrapped around 1000 B.C. Unlike normal X-ray images, xeroradiographs emphasize edges, so that outlines of shapes are easier to see. This is useful in identifying amulets (pp. 20–21) and wrapped organs, as well as bones and other body tissues. This image revealed a lot of packing material which was pushed under the skin to make the shrunken body more lifelike.

Arms by sides (not crossed over) with hands covering genitals

Edge of linen bandages

Atef crown of two feathers, a symbol of the god Osiris

Facial features painted on wrappings

Ear wrapped separately

MALE DANCER
This unusual mummy from Egypt's Roman period (pp. 42–43) was found lying in the coffin of a woman dating from much earlier. From the packing, which emphasizes the shapes of the breasts and thighs, it was assumed that the mummy was female. But X-rays taken in the 1960s revealed a man's body beneath the wrappings. The paintings on the linen represent body tattoos. He may have been a dancer who performed at religious ceremonies and banquets, because such dancers are known to have had similar tattoos. The embalmers wrapped the mummy with great care, packing it to give it the shape of a living body. The facial features were painted on, in the style of Old Kingdom mummies. The fingers and toes are all wrapped separately, even in the outer layers. This is very rare.

Elaborate geometric wrapping on forearms, typical of Roman period

Side view of Roman mummy, showing careful wrapping of individual fingers

Tattoo painted onto wrappings

Holes in skull

Badly bent bones

BONE DISEASE
This cartonnage coffin from the 22nd Dynasty (945–715 B.C.) once held the mummy of a child. All that remains of the body is a skeleton. Medical experts found that the strange deformities in the skull and other bones were caused by a rare bone disease called osteogenesis imperfecta. This would have afflicted the child while still in the mother's womb. He or she must have been born with brittle bones and probably died soon after.

Piece of jewelry inset in sandal

Linen sandals

MUMMY FINGERPRINT
Even after 3,000 years, it is still possible to take a mummy's fingerprints. Police forensic experts at Scotland Yard in London, England, have the prints of an Egyptian mummy in their records of modern criminals. They took the prints from a mummy's hand lent to them by the British Museum.

Continued on next page

Continued from previous page

ROYAL VISIT TO PARIS

In 1974, experts in Egypt discovered that Ramses II's skin was being destroyed by a mysterious infection. The royal mummy was flown to Paris three years later for medical treatment. International regulations required him to have a passport, which gave his occupation as "King (deceased)." When he arrived in France, a team of conservators successfully cured the infection, which turned out to be a fungus. A total of 102 specialists, including radiographers, police forensic scientists, botanists, and textile experts, examined the ancient pharaoh's body.

Nasal cavity stuffed with peppercorns

Small animal bone

Missing teeth

STUCK UP

This xeroradiograph (p. 49) revealed the secret of the mummy's dignified profile. The embalmers had kept the king's nose in the air by packing it with peppercorns and propping it with a tiny animal bone.

Ramses the Great revealed

The mummy of Ramses II was found in 1881 (p. 36) and has been resting in the Cairo Museum ever since. A special trip to Paris in 1977 gave medical experts from around the world a unique chance to examine the dead pharaoh's body. It is interesting to compare their findings with the historical records of his 67-year reign. X-rays showed a battle wound on one shoulder and signs of a healed fracture in one toe. The king may have suffered these injuries in an accident in the desert, an event described in ancient records. Close examination revealed a tiny piece of blue and gold fabric stuck to the mummy's skin. This was probably part of the king's clothes. Traces of unusual sand suggest that he may have been embalmed near Per-Ramesse, the king's northern capital. Analysis of resins identified the herbs and flowers used to embalm him. Ramses's body was especially rich in camomile oil. It was also coated with an extract from a wild tobacco plant, possibly added to keep insects off the body.

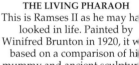

THE LIVING PHARAOH

This is Ramses II as he may ha looked in life. Painted by Winifred Brunton in 1920, it v based on a comparison of hi mummy and ancient sculptur There is a striking physical resemblance between Ramses his father, Seti I (p. 28), and k son, Merenptah. The mummie the three kings all have larg hooked noses.

REDHEAD

Considering he is more than 3, years old, Ramses II is in very good health. His hair was probably dyed with henna but seems to have been naturally r His slightly open mouth revea good set of teeth. Abscesses in jaw must have caused him grea pain. The king also suffered fr blood circulation problems and severe arthritis in the hips. This must have made it hard for hir get around in his last years. He was probably in his nineties w he died and had a bent back. T keep his head up, the embalme had to break his spine.

CAT scanning

Since 1977, doctors have been examining mummies with the help of an advanced X-ray process called CAT scanning. CAT stands for computerized axial tomography (the last word means "cut" or "section"). A normal X-ray produces one flat view of an object. But a CAT scan takes many thin views, each one like a slice of bread. These are then processed by a computer and put together to produce the whole loaf – a three-dimensional image of the object and all its surfaces, inside and out. It is possible to zoom in on one slice or isolate a particular part of the mummy to study it in more detail. The thickness of the slices can also be varied to give more information on one area like the skull or teeth. In 1991, doctors at St. Thomas's Hospital in London, England, began a mummy scanning program with the British Museum. The first mummy they studied was Tjentmutengebtiu, a priestess who died around 900 B.C. She is enclosed in a beautiful cartonnage case that would be damaged if it were opened.

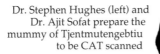

Cartonnage mummy case of Tjentmutengebtiu

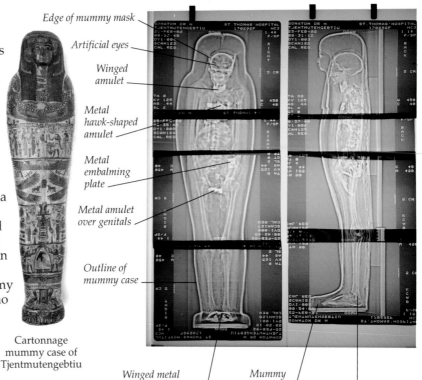

Edge of mummy mask

Artificial eyes

Winged amulet

Metal hawk-shaped amulet

Metal embalming plate

Metal amulet over genitals

Outline of mummy case

Winged metal amulet lying on feet

Mummy wrappings

Skeleton of mummy

X-RAY VIEWING

The CAT scanner can also simulate normal, flat X-ray images (above). Dense structures like bones are shown in white. Less dense materials like bandages come out dark blue or black. These X-rays show the skeleton inside the mummy and the mummy lying inside its case. The mummy mask, artificial eyes, various amulets, and an embalming plate can also be seen.

TV CELEBRITY
Radiographers view the scanning process on high resolution television screens in a separate observation booth. They can control the thickness of the individual slices. The radiographers took slices 0.1 in (2 mm) thick of Tjentmutengebtiu's head and neck and 0.2 in (4 mm) thick for the rest of her body. It took a total of over 500 slices to scan the mummy from head to toe.

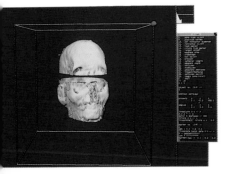

Dr. Stephen Hughes (left) and Dr. Ajit Sofat prepare the mummy of Tjentmutengebtiu to be CAT scanned

COMPUTER GRAPHICS
CAT scans tell doctors a lot about the density of objects hidden beneath the surface. Different tissues like bone or skin have their own distinctive densities. Once these have been calculated, one tissue can be isolated from the others. This is the skin on Tjentmutengebtiu's skull. The doctors can even look inside her skull and see details like the sinus cavities. Information on density can also reveal if an object like an amulet is made of clay or metal.

Mummies of the Andes

Dancing demon figure from Paracas, Peru, where many mummy bundles were found

— Helm

Mace —

Shie

THE EARLIEST MUMMIES FROM THE ANDES region of South America were made by fishing people who lived along the coasts of Chile and Peru. By 3000 B.C., they were preserving their dead by drying them in the sun and sometimes removing their internal organs, too. Mummies from various later cultures have been found all over modern Colombia, Ecuador, Peru, and Chile, from the high mountain peaks to the dry coastal lowlands. Many of these cultures treated the mummies of their ancestors as sacred objects. The Incas, who ruled most of the Andes region when the Europeans arrived in A.D. 1532, believed their dead king was a god. By worshiping his mummy, they hoped to keep his soul alive. A dead king's mummy was seated on a throne and looked after by attendants who fed and clothed him. On important religious days, the royal mummies were carried through the streets of the Inca capital, Cuzco.

POTTERY WARRIOR

The Moche were a farming an fishing people who lived on th northern coast of Peru from 200 B.C. to about A.D. 600. The made beautiful pottery to bur with their dead.

WILD CAT GOD

Cloth was highly valued by the ancient Peruvians. They were great weavers and embroiderers who regarded cloth as a form of wealth. This tapestry of a cat god was woven by the Chancay people (A.D. 1000–1470). The Chancay did not have pet cats, so it must represent a wild cat like the puma or jaguar. Great quantities of colorful fabric were sealed inside tombs. Mummies were also wrapped in many layers of cloth specially made for the purpose. Fine-quality garments were believed to show a person's importance. Weavers must have spent several years making the fabric for the most splendid mummies. Some burials even included cloth-making tools like looms, spindles, and thread.

Upper lip caught on tooth

Rope used to bundle body up

UNWRAPPED PERUVIAN MUMMY

Some Peruvian mummies were careful embalmed. This involved removing the internal organs, smoke-drying the body and rubbing it with oils, resins, and herb But most mummies were preserved by natural conditions – either the hot dry climate of the coast or the freezing cold the Andes Mountains. The drying proce was probably helped by the layers of fabric, which helped draw off the bod fluids. The dead person was usually placed in a sitting position with the knees drawn up against the chest. T hands were flattened over the face, and the arms and legs were bound tightly in place.

DESERT CEMETERY

The dry climate of the Peruvian coast was ideal for drying out mummies. In the 1880s, several hundred well-preserved mummies were found among the thousands of graves in the vast desert cemetery at Ancón. The high levels of natural salts in the soil seem to have helped preserve the bodies, including the mummies of pet dogs.

Well-preserved toenails

Male figure   Female figu

FERTILITY OFFERINGS

The Chancay people placed pottery with the dead. These hollow figures of a man and a woman stood on either side of a mummy. Th were probably once wrapped in bright textil

FALSE HEAD

This is a false head worn by one of the mummies found at Ancón, Peru, in the 1880s. It is like a cushion made of painted cotton stuffed with leaves or seaweed. The nose and mouth are carved wood. The eyes are shells, with small drops of resin for pupils. The hair is made of plant fiber dyed black. This is wrapped in a headband and crowned with a headdress made of brilliant green parrot feathers. In ancient Peru, such headdresses were a sign of high status.

False head

Copper eyes

Copper nose and mouth

Feather eyelashes

MUMMY BUNDLE
The Chimu were a highly developed farming people from northern Peru. Their kingdom flourished from A.D. 1000 until 1476, when they were conquered by the Incas. This is a Chimu mummy bundle with a false head. It contains a crouching body wrapped in many layers of fine cotton and wool cloth. X-rays revealed that the dead person's eyes were covered by plates of metal, probably gold. A bracelet was also seen on one wrist, and shells had been placed at the mummy's heels.

Striped mantle (cloak)

Belt from which pouches hang

HIGH IN THE ANDES
A side view shows the pouches that hang from a belt around the mummy's middle. They contain avocado seeds, raw cotton, and coca leaves, which the Chimu chewed to relax. These leaves contain the drug cocaine.

Pouch

Continued on next page

False head

Wig of long strands of human hair

Leaf packing

Animal skin

Mantle

PARACAS NECKLACE
This cloth necklace was found in the desolate Paracas Peninsula, on Peru's south coast. Hundreds of mummies dating from 1000 to 200 B.C. have been found in ancient cemeteries there.

Tiny human figures

SACRED DOLL
Found in the Pacasmayo Valley in Peru, this doll is made from woven tapestry, cloth, and reeds. She is holding a bundle of raw cotton. Cotton was one of the first crops to be grown in the Andes, and evidence of it goes back to 3000 B.C. The doll may be a goddess buried with a dead person to bring him or her luck.

INSIDE THE BUNDLE
This cross-section of a mummy bundle was drawn during the excavations of Ancón, Peru, in the 1880s. The mummy was found with a few vases in a grave about 10 ft (3 m) deep. Its false head includes a wig of human hair. Beneath the layers of colorful cloth, the dried body had been wrapped in an animal skin and tied up tightly.

Feathered headdress

Plaited hair band

SNAKE EMBROIDERY
The Paracas Peninsula is famous for its ancient textiles, found either with or as part of mummy bundles. Some bundles contained over 100 cotton garments. Shirts, mantles (cloaks), ponchos, skirts, loincloths, and turbans have all been found. Many of them are embroidered in wool with birds, animals, fish, and imaginary beasts.

Silver plate held between teeth

Cotton wrapping

Matting of raffia, a kind of palm

Stirrup spout

Turban

Ear spools

Feathered vest

BUNDLED UP
The Chancay culture flourished on the central coast of Peru from c. 1000 to 1470. When ordinary Chancas died, they were wrapped in plain cloth and buried in simple pits with a few goods. But the rich were buried in great tombs, some with stairs leading down to them. These contained many rooms full of beautiful gifts. This Chanca woman was probably wrapped in palm matting. She is wearing clothes of cotton and feathers. Her mouth was packed with llama wool and sealed with a silver plate.

MOCHE STIRRUP POT
The Moche made fine pottery vessels and figures to put in tombs. They even used clay molds to mass-produce favorite designs. The pots often have spouts shaped like stirrups. The head of a Moche lord forms the body of this pot. His earlobes are stretched and he wears the large ear spools worn by important Moche men.

Pair of gold ear spools

Sandals made of raffia fiber

SILENT SCREAM
Mexican museums contain many ancient mummies like this one. More recent preserved bodies have become tourist attractions. The gruesome mummies on display in Guanajuato, a vast cemetery in Mexico City, are all from the 20th century.

Sewn-up eyes

Sewn-up mouth

SHRUNKEN HEAD
The Jivaro Indians of the Amazon were among the many groups of people who used to shrink their enemies' heads. They believed a person's soul lived in the head. By owning an enemy's head, a Jivaro warrior could possess some of the dead person's spiritual strength. The Jivaro shrunk the heads to less than half their original size in an elaborate process that lasted six days. They then decorated the hair, which did not shrink, with beads and feathers. The result was a *tsantsa*, or trophy head. Warriors wore *tsantsas* around their necks at special festivals.

Plaited hair

Other American mummies
Mummies have been found in many parts of the American continent, from Argentina in the south to as far north as Alaska. Some of the earliest bodies, from the first century B.C., come from the Kentucky region. Most of these mummies have been found in caves, like the bodies of Navahos in Arizona. The freezing cold has preserved the tattooed bodies of Inuit in Alaska. The inhabitants of the nearby Aleutian Islands buried their dead in warm volcanic caves, which helped to dry them out. Some of the bodies found here were stuffed with dry grass after the insides were removed. In South America, mummies have been found in many places beyond Peru. The Jivaro Indians of the Amazon even shrunk the severed heads of their enemies.

CHILEAN GIRL
At its height, the empire of the Incas stretched from Ecuador in the north to Bolivia and Chile in the south. This is the freeze-dried mummy of an Incan girl found high in the Andes in Chile. The Incas practiced human sacrifice. During droughts or other times of crisis, children were sometimes selected, with their parents' approval, to be mummified and offered to the gods. When a king died, some of his favorite wives and servants were killed. They were then mummified so they could accompany the dead king on his journey to the next world.

COLOMBIAN MUMMY
This mummy of a woman was found with 13 others in a cave near Bogotá, in the Colombian Andes. She is wearing a necklace of animal teeth and pieces of carved sea shell. Her internal organs were removed through an incision at the base of the spine. Her hands were then tied across her chest, after which her body may have been smoke-dried.

Mark of tightly wrapped cloth on skin

Badly worn teeth

Dry, papery skin

55

The Iceman

THE DISCOVERY

On September 19, 1991, two German climbers found a body frozen in the top of a glacier. It was about 10,000 ft (3,000 m) up in a remote part of the Alps near the Austrian-Italian border. The body had been partly uncovered because of a freak storm in the Sahara Desert in March. This had blown great clouds of dust over the Alps and onto the glacier. The dark dust absorbed the sunlight and made the ice melt more than usual. The police and forensic experts who arrived on the scene didn't realize the body was so old. They hacked it out of the ice (above) and flew it by helicopter to Innsbruck, Austria, to be examined. At first it seemed that he was Austrian, and Austria has become the center of Iceman research. But surveyors later found that the body had lain just inside the modern Italian border.

ONE AUTUMN DAY OVER 5,300 YEARS AGO, an exhausted traveler was surprised by a sudden snowstorm high in the Alps. He took shelter in a gully between two ridges of rock. But the storm was fierce, and he died from exposure and cold where he lay. Snow covered his body, and he was soon frozen into a glacier. Winters came and went, centuries passed, the empires of Egypt, Greece, and Rome rose and fell. Europe was ravaged by two world wars, but still the dead man lay frozen in time, until freak weather in the summer of 1991 exposed his body once again. After it had been found, a technique called radiocarbon dating was used to estimate the body's age. It showed that the Iceman, as he is now known, died between 3350 and 3300 B.C. This makes him the oldest well-preserved mummy in the world. More than 70 objects were found with him. They are not grave goods, but personal possessions he was carrying when he died. Teams of specialists are now studying the Iceman's body, clothing, tools, and weapons. Botanists are examining the plant matter found on his body, which may show where he was from. His blood, bones, vital organs, and DNA may reveal the diseases he suffered from. All of this research may give clues to who the Iceman was, and how he lived and died.

RADIOCARBON DATING

Robert Hedges works at the Radiocarbon Unit at Oxford University in England. He developed a new method of radiocarbon dating, which he used to prove that the Turin Shroud was a fake (far right). Radiocarbon dating works because all organic (living) things contain a molecule called carbon-14. This disappears at a constant rate after they die. So by measuring the level of carbon-14, scientists can calculate the age of any organic substance. Hedges dated the Iceman by testing a small bone sample. His results shocked experts, who had guessed that the Iceman had died around 2000 B.C.

SHROUD OF TURIN

People once believed that the body of Christ was wrapped in this relic. But radiocarbon tests showed that it was made in the Middle Ages.

Leather quiver

Wooden ax with copper head

Part of leather shoe lined with grass, still stuck on foot

ARMS AND THE ICEMAN

Some of the items the Iceman was carrying are extraordinary. There was a bow and a leather quiver holding 12 half-made arrows. His ax looks like a typical Bronze Age model from about 2000 B.C., but it turned out to be copper. It is an amazing tool, much older and more advanced in design than any known copper ax.

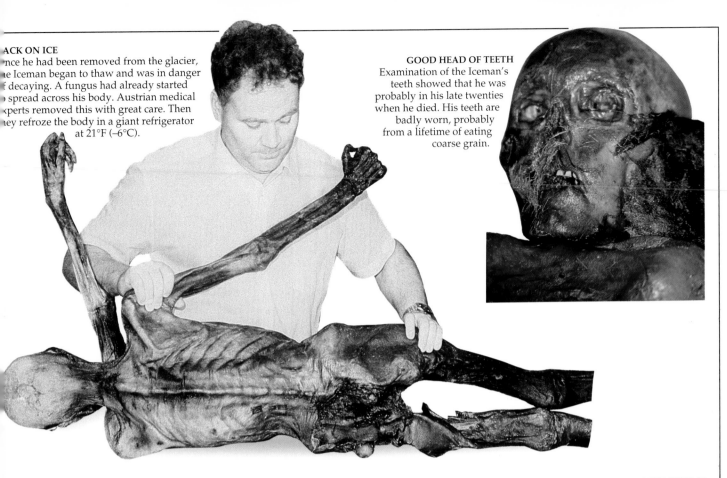

BACK ON ICE

Once he had been removed from the glacier, the Iceman began to thaw and was in danger of decaying. A fungus had already started to spread across his body. Austrian medical experts removed this with great care. Then they refroze the body in a giant refrigerator at 21°F (–6°C).

GOOD HEAD OF TEETH

Examination of the Iceman's teeth showed that he was probably in his late twenties when he died. His teeth are badly worn, probably from a lifetime of eating coarse grain.

FROZEN IN TIME

So who was the Iceman? He was at least 5 ft 2 in (1.57 m) tall and had several strange tattoos. He was once well dressed for the mountains in patched leather clothes and shoes stuffed with grass for extra warmth. He also had a grass bag and cape. He was carrying an ax, a bow and arrows, and a flint scraper in a leather pouch, which may have been a kit for starting fires. What was he doing with all this gear so high in the mountains? He may have been a hunter or a traveler from a farming town on a trading mission. It is not clear in what direction he was crossing the Alps. He may have come from one of several known towns in Italy, Austria, or southern Germany.

Bog mummies

LINDOW WOMAN
In 1983, two peat workers stumbled upon a partly decomposed female head in the same bog in Cheshire, England where Lindow Man (p. 59) was later found. A local man soon confessed that he had murdered his wife and dumped her in the bog 23 years earlier. He was tried and found guilty of murder. But when the head was radiocarbon dated, it was found to be over 1,770 years old!

SOME ANCIENT BODIES have been found in wet, marshy places such as bogs. They are often found by people cutting peat (decomposed plant matter that has been burned as a fuel for centuries). The discovery of a body in a bog usually attracts the attention of the police, who assume that someone has had an accident or been murdered recently. Only after the body has been radiocarbon dated (p. 56) can scientists tell how long ago the person died. The best bog mummies have been found in northern Europe, especially Denmark. They date from the late Iron Age, as early as 500 B.C., to the Roman period, up to A.D. 400. These well-preserved corpses have a number of things in common, and archaeologists believe they are from a similar culture. The victims were all killed on dry land and then thrown into the bog. They may have been executed as punishment for some crime, or as a human sacrifice to the gods. Their many injuries even suggest that the victims were executed in some religious ritual. Forensic evidence suggests that they all died in midwinter, so this may have been a festival celebrated at that time.

Severed arm

HULDRE FEN WOMA
This bog woman was foun over 100 years ago i Huldre Fen in Denmar! She died about A.D. 9. Most bog bodies ar naked, but she wa wearing a lambski cape and a checke skirt and hea scarf. A finel crafted horn com and a string with tw amber beads were als found with her. Thi suggests that she was n poor and may have held a important position in society. N one knows if her arm was cut o before or after she die

The hair of many mummies seems to have turned red over the years

Scar from cut throat

GRAUBALLE MAN
This body of a man was found near Grauballe, Denmark, in 1952. At first he was thought to be a drunken peat worker known as Red Christian, who had fallen into the bog way back in 1887. But he is now known to have died between 1,540 and 1,740 years ago. After it had been taken out of the bog, the body had to be treated to stop it from deteriorating. It was placed in a strong solution of oak bark and slowly tanned over 18 months. Grauballe Man is incredibly well preserved, with most of his internal organs intact. Even his fingerprints could be studied (p. 49). The contents of his stomach told scientists what he had eaten for his last meal. He seems to have had a vegetable soup which contained barley and a sort of muesli made from the seeds of over 60 different plants. He died violently, from many injuries, including a cut throat.

Long, narrow hand

Leathery skin, naturally tanned in peat bog

OVERKILL
Lindow Man seems to have been killed by several methods. A knotted cord was found embedded in his neck. It seems to have been used to choke or strangle him. His throat was also cut, and his skull was caved in by heavy blows. All this "overkill" suggests that his death was a sacrifice or some kind of religious ceremony.

Fragile hair, including a beard, rarely found on bog bodies

Cord used to choke or strangle him

GREEING ON A DATE
ogs contain little oxygen. This stops bacteria, which cause ecay, from growing (p. 8). How well a body is preserved so depends on how cold the water is and how eeply the body is submerged. A team of chaeologists and other specialists moved Lindow Man from the peat. hey then took samples from the ody and the peat and sent them three research laboratories to be ated by the radiocarbon method. hough their results were not entical, the experts eventually agreed that e Lindow Man had ed around 300 B.C.

Ulna, one of the bones in the forearm

Fingernail resting on skin

Fragments of bones from right hand

HAT DID HE LOOK LIKE?
indow Man must have looked a lot better 300 years ago. But his face was distorted ver the centuries as he lay crumpled in is wet grave. This was a challenge for cientists who try and reconstruct faces to elp the police to identify human remains. hey based their calculations on careful easurements of the skull, allowing for the ickness of skin and muscle. The fine ondition of his fingernails shows that indow Man didn't work with his hands, and may even have been a chieftain.

Navel

Tough, leathery skin

Lindow Man

In 1984, peat cutters found a man's body in a bog at Lindow Moss in Cheshire, England. The discovery that he was about 2,300 years old made the dead man famous overnight. Newspapers gave him the nickname Pete Marsh, a pun on the type of bog he was found in. Scientific research revealed many interesting details about his body. Examination of his teeth suggests he was between 25 and 30 years old when he died. He was in good health, but suffered from intestinal worms. The contents of his stomach showed that his last meal was a high-fiber mixture of cereal, bran, and slightly burnt bread.

The mummies of Sicily

ABOUT 6,000 MUMMIES are still resting in a catacomb (underground cemetery) beneath a Catholic church in Palermo, the capital of the Italian island of Sicily. The first mummies, nearly 400 years old, are of monks who lived and worshiped in the church.

The custom soon became fashionable with doctors, lawyers, and other rich professionals in Palermo. The monks embalmed the bodies themselves, in a secret process that took more than a year. Like the ancient Egyptians, the Sicilians didn't find their mummies disturbing. They saw the preserved bodies as a direct link with their dead relatives, whose spirits were enjoying the afterlife. Families took their children to visit their great-grandparents, long after they had passed away. Visitors brought picnics on their outings to the catacombs. The families would pray and talk to the mummies, keep them up-to-date on local affairs, and ask their advice on difficult matters. No one has been mummified here for over 70 years, but the monks are still kept busy giving tours to visitors.

FOUNDING FATHER
The oldest mummy in the catacombs Father Silvestro da Gubbio, embalme in 1599. First, his body was carrie down to a special cellar, the *collat* Here it was laid on earthenware pipe and left for 12 months, until all th body fluids had drained away. It wa then taken upstairs and left to dry the sunshine. Before it was dresse the body was washed in vineg and wrapped in straw an sweet-smelling herb

BEARDED GUARDIANS
The monks live over the catacombs and are in charge of the mummies and all the cemetery records. They belong to the Capuchin order. All Capuchin monks have beards and wear robes with hoods.

DRESSED IN SUNDAY'S BEST
These mummies of women are all from a part of the catacombs known as the Corridor of the Virgins. Their costumes are a remarkable historical record of dress-making skills and textile design. The lacework is particularly impressive. The coffins the bodies lie in are hinged, so relatives could hold hands with the mummies while they prayed.

Well-preserved, colorful clothes

Labels with details like the dead person's name, age, and profession

MILKY SOFT
In the 19th century, a new, better method of embalming was developed. The monks began to soak the bodies in arsenic or milk of magnesia, which left the skin softer and more lifelike.

DUSTY DEATH
There are now fewer than 40 monks looking after the 6,000 mummies. Every year, they give the dead bodies a gentle clean with a vacuum cleaner.

Clothes of cotton, which has worn less than silk

Sicilian mummy with head propped up on pillow

SLEEPING BEAUTY
Rosali Lombardo, the last Sicilian to be mummified, died at the age of two in 1920. Her body was preserved by a unique process developed by her father, who was a doctor.

Other mummies

NATURAL MUMMIES ARE PRESERVED by accident (pp. 8–9), and are found anywhere in the world where it is cold, dry, or marshy enough. Australian aborigines, Torres Strait Islanders, and native South and North Americans all used natural conditions to preserve bodies deliberately. In Christian churches and Buddhist temples, holy people are sometimes mummified and put on display (pp. 7, 60–61). Every year, the mummy of a Christian saint is carried through the streets in a great procession in a town in Crete. In the 20th century, people began to mummify famous politicians and celebrities rather than kings and saints. Improved methods of embalming involving paraffin wax were developed in Argentina. In 1952, these were used to preserve beautifully the body of the president's wife, Eva Perón. In Salt Lake City, Utah, you can now pay to have a dead relative or pet embalmed and wrapped in the ancient Egyptian way.

GUANCHE MUMMIES
In 1770, a volcanic cave containing about 1,000 mummies was found on Tenerife, one of the Canary Islands. They belonged to the Guanche people, who had been preserving their dead for centuries. Their method of embalming was remarkably like the Egyptian way. In some cases the Guanches removed the internal organs. Then they dried the body and stuffed it with plants. Few Guanche mummies have survived, because so many were ground up to make medicines.

Wax head

Real head

AUTO ICON
When the English philosopher Jeremy Bentham died in 1832, he left his body to a surgeon friend. According to his instructions, his head was mummified. His skeleton was then dressed in his everyday clothes and crowned with a wax head. The whole ensemble is still displayed in a glass case in University College, London. Bentham called it his "Auto Icon" (self-image).

Sealskin trousers

Outer parka made of sealskin trimmed with fur

FISHY MUMMY
Mermaids (and, more rarely, mermen) were popular curiosities in Europe as early as the 17th century. These imaginary creatures mostly came from East Asia, especially Japan. This mummified merman was made from a monkey's body and a fish's tail. Seijiro Arisuye, who gave it to an English prince, claimed that it had been caught by a Japanese fisherman.

Kamik, sealskin boots

LADY DAI, HER TRUE STORY

Lady Dai was a Chinese noblewoman from the Han dynasty who died around 168 B.C. Her well-preserved body was found in a deep tomb in Hunan province in 1972. She was wrapped in layers of silk and lay in a nest of six wooden coffins, all beautifully painted. These were covered in many layers of bamboo matting and five tons of charcoal. This was probably designed to soak up any water and keep the body perfectly dry. The tomb was then sealed with dirt and clay to keep it airtight. Examination of her body showed that Lady Dai had been embalmed by soaking in a bath of mercury salts.

Lady Dai being X-rayed

2,160 pieces of nephrite, a kind of jade, linked with gold wires

SUN-DRIED

This New Guinean is posing proudly with a mummified ancestor. In hot parts of the world, many people used to place bodies in the branches of trees to be dried by the sun. The islanders of the Torres Strait, between Australia and New Guinea, would tie a dead body to a bamboo stretcher. Then they would light a fire under it and smoke it dry. Finally they painted the body with red ocher.

JADED SUIT

A Chinese princess from the second century B.C. was buried in this beautiful jade suit. She had hoped that the gemstone would mummify her. But under the jade, her body decayed anyway.

FROZEN SCYTHIANS

The Scythians were nomads who lived in central Asia from the seventh to the third century B.C. They mummified their dead chiefs and nobles with as much care as the ancient Egyptians. They removed the internal organs and stuffed the body with frankincense, parsley, and hair. This picture of a Scythian horseman is part of a textile buried with a chief. The Scythians spent most of their lives on horseback, and chiefs were even buried with their mummified horses. Warriors were tattooed for their bravery, and one chief has elaborate tattoos all over his body. Their burial mounds in Siberia were freezing cold, which helped to preserve the bodies.

DRESSED IN FURS

This mummy of an Inuit woman is one of eight well-preserved bodies found in Greenland in 1972 (p. 7). She died around 1475 at the age of 30. The combination of dry air and freezing temperatures naturally freeze-dried her body. Her warm clothing, all hand-made from animal skins, was also well preserved. The Inuit believed that a dead person's soul would need warm clothes for the long voyage to "The Land of the Dead." Infrared photographs revealed faded tattoos on her face. Four of the other five women buried with her had similar tattoos.

Inner parka made of bird skin

Did you know?

AMAZING FACTS

The Chancay people from South America often placed doll-like figures in their tombs to serve the dead person in the afterlife, much like Egyptian shabti figures.

Chancay doll

Canopic jars, used to store a mummy's internal organs, are named after the local god of Canopus, a town in the Nile delta region. He was represented as a human-headed pot.

The ancient Egyptians believed that the land of the dead lay in the west, where the sun set, so most of their cemeteries, including the Valley of the Kings, were situated on the west bank of the Nile River. One of the names for Osiris, the god of the dead, was "Foremost of the Westerners."

The Egyptian god Osiris

The Valley of the Kings is situated on the west bank of the Nile.

In ancient Egypt, a body being mummified was placed on a slanted bed and covered with a form of salt called natron for 40 days. At the end of this period, the body would have shrunk in size and lost about 75 percent of its original weight, thanks to the dehydrating effect of the natron.

The frozen bodies of sailors from Sir John Franklin's 1845 Arctic expedition were so well preserved that scientists were able to carry out post-mortems in 1985. The results suggested that lead poisoning, caused by eating faultily canned food, may have caused the mental and physical decline of the crew.

Egyptologists gained useful information about the process of mummification from an account in the Bible. In the book of Genesis, Jacob dies in Egypt and his son Joseph has his body embalmed. "So the physicians embalmed him, taking a full 40 days, for that was the time required for embalming. And the Egyptians mourned him for 70 days." (Genesis 50:2-3). These 40 and 70–day periods confirmed another account given by the Greek historian Herodotus.

Vast amounts of linen were used to wrap an ancient Egyptian mummy. When experts at the Metropolitan Museum of Art in New York measured how much linen had been used on one mummy from the 11th dynasty, they found that it totaled an amazing 1,010 square yards (845 square meters). That's enough linen to cover three tennis courts!

During mummification, the internal organs were removed through a long incision on the left side of the body. The line of the cut was marked by one priest, called a "scribe," then a second priest, appropriately known as the "slicer" or "ripper up," made the cut with a flint knife.

During the Middle Ages, mummies were in great demand in Europe for use as medicine. Large numbers of them were imported from Egypt for this purpose. One common use was to boil a mummy and then skim off the melted oils to make an ointment to prevent bruising. Mummy was also used as an ingredient in potions to treat stomach upsets and many other illnesses.

The Valley of the Kings was said to be protected by a goddess called Meretseger, who took the form of a cobra. The tomb workers believed that she would blind or poison any robbers who tampered with the tombs.

The goddess Meretseger in the form of a cobra

QUESTIONS AND ANSWERS

Step Pyramid

Q Why were early Egyptian pharaohs buried in pyramid-shaped tombs?

A The earliest pyramid was the Step Pyramid, built as the burial place of King Djoser in c. 2650 BCE. Its shape was supposed to represent a giant stairway for the dead king to climb to join the sun god in the sky. Later pyramids had sloping sides. This shape represented the mound that, according to Egyptian legend, had emerged from the watery ground at the beginning of time. The sun god stood on this mound and brought the other gods and goddesses into being.

Q Why didn't the Egyptians remove a mummy's heart?

A Egyptian embalmers removed most of a mummy's internal organs, but the heart was always left in place. The Egyptians believed that the dead person would need his or her heart when judged in the afterlife (see p. 13). It was therefore essential that the heart be kept with the body, and it was often protected by a powerful amulet, called the heart scarab.

Anubis, jackal-headed god of embalming

Egyptian god Anubis

Q Why was the Egyptian god Anubis associated with mummification?

A Real jackals often roamed the graveyards of ancient Egypt, so this is probably why Anubis, the jackal-headed god, came to be the god of embalming and the guardian of the dead. He was often depicted with black skin, because for the Egyptians the color black represented the fertile Nile mud and therefore life itself.

Q Are bodies still being mummified today?

A Yes, but in different ways. You can have your dead pet mummified, and some wealthy people have their bodies preserved using a form of deep freezing called cryonics.

Q Were the dead always treated with respect?

A Egyptian embalmers were not always as careful as they should have been when preparing mummies. We know of one mummy whose head was snapped off and reattached to the body with a stick, and a queen whose face was so stuffed with pads of linen that it split away from her head. But once the bodies were wrapped in bandages, the grieving family could not see these mistakes.

Q What happened to Egyptian tomb robbers if they were caught?

A Egyptian pharaohs were buried with such vast amounts of treasure that their tombs inevitably attracted robbers. If they were lucky and escaped undetected, tomb robbers could make quick profits from selling their loot, but if they were caught, they faced a terrible fate. First they would be tortured by having the soles of their feet beaten with rods. Then they would suffer an agonizing public death, impaled on a sharp wooden stake.

Q Which animals were mummified?

A The ancient Egyptians mummifed all sorts of animals—cats, rams, ibises, hawks, and crocodiles were among the most common. But mice, rats, lizards, and even a mummified egg have also been found.

Record Breakers

OLDEST MUMMY
The body of the Iceman was preserved in a glacier in the Alps for more than 5,300 years, making him the oldest mummy yet discovered.

MISSING MUMMY
In 1818, the Italian archaeologist Giovanni Belzoni entered the burial chamber of the Great Pyramid. He discovered that it had been robbed, and there was no sign of the mummy of Pharaoh Khufu. The mummy has never been found.

RICHEST MUMMY
Not only was Tutankhamun the only royal mummy discovered with its priceless treasures intact, but his treasures continued to earn vast amounts of money when they went on tour around the world during the 1960s and 1970s. The exhibition was so popular that visitors often lined up for hours to see it.

MOST POPULAR MUMMY?
Millions of visitors to Moscow have been to see the mummified body of the Russian leader Vladimir Lenin, making him one of the city's most popular tourist attractions.

The world's oldest mummy was discovered in the Alps.

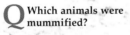

Timeline

THE PRESERVATION of dead bodies by mummification has been happening for centuries. Sometimes it is accidental, caused by favorable weather conditions, while others have been deliberately preserved by people. The mummies in this book span more than 5,000 years, from the Iceman, who died around 3350 BCE, to Lenin, whose body was mummified in the 1920s. This timeline shows you who was mummified when.

These figures were probably a mother and child

Casts of two bodies, whose shapes were preserved in the ash at Pompeii

C. 3350–3300 BCE EUROPE
A traveler later known as the Iceman dies of exposure and cold in the Alps. His body is frozen into a glacier.

C. 3200 BCE EGYPT
The oldest surviving Egyptian mummies date from this period. They are bodies buried in the desert sand, which dries and mummifies them naturally.

C. 3000 BCE SOUTH AMERICA
People along the coasts of Chile and Peru start preserving the bodies of their dead by drying them in the sun.

2686–2160 BCE EGYPT
During the Old Kingdom, mummies of kings and queens are buried in pyramids. Mummies of less famous people are buried in rectangular coffins.

A 2,000-year-old mummy from Peru, preserved by dry conditions

C. 2000 BCE EGYPT
The Egyptians start embalming some of the body's internal organs separately and storing them in canopic jars. The first mummiform (mummy-shaped) coffins are used.

1492 BCE EGYPT
Death of Pharaoh Tuthmosis I, the first pharaoh to build his tomb in the Valley of the Kings.

1324 BCE EGYPT
Death of the boy pharaoh Tutankhamun. He is buried in a small tomb in the Valley of the Kings.

C. 1000 BCE EGYPT
Egyptian priests collect a number of royal mummies from tombs in the Valley of the Kings that have been disturbed by robbers. They rebury them in two secret hiding places called caches.

450 BCE EGYPT
The Greek historian Herodotus visits Egypt and writes an eyewitness account of the mummification process.

C. 300 BCE ENGLAND
A man is sacrificed during a religious ceremony and his corpse is thrown into a bog at Lindow Moss in Cheshire.

CE 79 ITALY
Mount Vesuvius erupts, burying the nearby towns of Pompeii and Herculaneum under volcanic rock and ash. The ash forms a hard crust around each body. Once the bodies decompose, empty body-shaped spaces are left in their place.

CE C. 1000–1476 SOUTH AMERICA
The Chimu people rule northern Peru. They mummify their dead and bury them in mummy bundles.

CE C. 1100–1532 SOUTH AMERICA
The Inca people rule an empire stretching from modern-day Ecuador to Chile and Bolivia. They bury their dead in the Andes Mountains. The bodies are mummified by the cold, which freeze-dries them.

Mummy of an Inuit child, preserved by dry air and cold temperatures

CE C. 1475 GREENLAND
The bodies of eight Inuit people are freeze-dried by dry air and freezing temperatures. They are not discovered until 1972.

CE 1599 ITALY
Monks at a church in Palermo, Sicily, start mummifying the bodies of monks who die. The practice continues until the 1920s.

Mummified bodies in a church
in Palermo, Italy

CE 1798 EGYPT
Napoleon Bonaparte invades Egypt.
French scholars remove many mummy
cases from their tombs and send them
to Paris.

19TH CENTURY CE JAPAN
The bodies of some Buddhist priests
are mummified by smoke-drying.

Engraving of Sir John Franklin's
expedition to the Arctic

CE 1845 THE ARCTIC
Sir John Franklin leads an expedition
along the northern coast of Canada,
looking for a route to the Pacific. Franklin
and his men are never seen alive again.

CE 1880s SOUTH AMERICA
Several hundred ancient Peruvian
mummies are found in a vast desert
cemetery at Ancon.

CE 1881 EGYPT
A cache of royal mummies is discovered
at Deir el-Bahari, near the Valley of the
Kings. It contains 40 royal mummies,
including the famous pharaohs
Seti I and Ramses II.

CE 1898 EGYPT
A second cache of mummies is discovered
in the Valley of the Kings in the tomb of
Amenhotep II. It contains 16 mummies,
10 of them royal.

20TH CENTURY CE MEXICO
Large numbers of mummified bodies
are buried in the Guanajuato cemetery
in Mexico City.

CE 1922 EGYPT
Archaeologist Howard
Carter discovers the tomb
of Tutankhamun in the
Valley of the Kings. It
contains many treasures
and his mummy—the
only pharaoh's
mummy ever found
undisturbed in
its tomb.

CE 1924 RUSSIA
Death of the Russian
revolutionary leader
Vladimir Lenin. His
body is preserved
using paraffin wax
and displayed in Red
Square, Moscow.

CE 1950 DENMARK
The 2,000-year-old
body of a man is
discovered preserved in
the Tollund bog.

CE 1977 FRANCE
The mummy of
Pharaoh Ramses II is
taken to Paris
for x-rays and
other tests.

CE 1984 THE ARCTIC
The bodies of three sailors from Sir John
Franklin's expedition are discovered in
the Canadian Arctic. The icy conditions
have preserved their bodies intact.

CE 1984 UK
The body of Lindow Man is discovered
preserved in the Lindow Moss bog. The
body has lain there for 2,300 years, but
scientists are able to establish how he
died, how old he was, and what he ate
for his last meal.

CE 1991 EUROPE
Freak weather conditions in the Alps
expose the body of the Iceman. Scientists
use radiocarbon dating to establish that
the body has been frozen in the ice for
more than 5,300 years.

Mummified body of Lenin

MAIN PERIODS IN EGYPTIAN HISTORY

The civilization of ancient Egypt lasted for
more than 3,000 years. Historians divide
this huge length of time into various
periods, which are listed below. They
also group the pharaohs into "families"
of related kings, called dynasties.

c. 3100–2686 BCE Early Dynastic Period
1st–2nd dynasties

c. 2686–2181 BCE Old Kingdom
3rd–6th dynasties

c. 2181–2055 BCE 1st Intermediate Period
7th–11th dynasties

c. 2055–1650 BCE Middle Kingdom
11th–14th dynasties

c. 1650–1550 BCE 2nd Intermediate Period
15th–17th dynasties

c. 1550–1069 BCE New Kingdom
18th–20th dynasties

c. 1069–715 BCE 3rd Intermediate Period
21st–24th dynasties

c. 715–332 BCE Late Period
25th–30th dynasties

c. 332–30 BCE Ptolemaic Period
Macedonian and Ptolemaic dynasties

Find out more

IF YOU ARE LUCKY ENOUGH to go on a trip to Egypt, you will have no trouble seeing lots of mummies, and you will also be able to visit the pyramids and tombs where they were buried. But you don't have to travel that far to find out more about mummies. Many museums in this country have mummies from Egypt and South America on display, so check out museums near you to see if they have a mummy collection. Alternatively, you could unwrap the secrets of mummies in your own home. Try visiting some of the exciting Web sites devoted to mummies, and keep an eye open for documentaries about mummies on television.

Headdress of the ram-headed god, Khnum

Visitors inspecting a mummy in the Egyptian Museum, Cairo

VISITING EGYPT
Many famous royal mummies now lie in the Egyptian Museum in Cairo, while the Mummification Museum at Luxor is home to many human and animal mummies. Another site worth visiting is the Serapeum, near the Pyramids at Giza, where the mummified bodies of the Apis Bulls were buried.

THE VALLEY OF THE KINGS
Archaeologists have uncovered more than 80 tombs in the Valley of the Kings, many of which you can visit. Unfortunately, most of the mummies are long gone. Some were removed by tomb robbers an others have ended up in museums Today, Tutankhamun's mummy is the only one still lying in its tomb.

Publicity poster for a recent movie featuring mummies

THE EGYPTIAN MUSEUM
In the Royal Mummy Room of the Egyptian Museum in Cairo you can see the mummies of Ramses II, Seti I, and many other famous pharaohs. The museum also houses a collection of animal mummies, such as this ram.

Mummy case for a mummified ram

MOVIES AND TELEVISION DOCUMENTARIES
One of the best ways to keep up to date with the world of mummies is to watch documentaries on television. These often feature the latest archaeological finds, and you may well be able to watch a mummy being scanned or even unwrapped. You may also enjoy movies featuring mummies, but beware—these are not always strictly historically accurate!

Many of the Valley tombs are beautifully decorated with wall paintings like this scene from the tomb of Seti I.

Cartouche

These hieroglyphs appear on an obelisk at Luxor.

HIEROGLYPHICS

Many ancient Egyptian mummy cases are covered with inscriptions. Hieroglyphics are difficult to learn to read, but one thing you can look for is an oval shape, called a cartouche. This was only used to surround the hieroglyphs making up a pharaoh's name. So if you see a cartouche, it tells you that the mummy was a pharaoh.

VISITING A MUSEUM

Some museums with the most extensive collections are shown in the box on the right, but many other museums around the world do contain mummies. In addition to the mummies themselves, museums often display information about X-rays and CAT scans performed on their mummies and what objects may be hidden inside the mummies' wrappings.

Places to Visit

MUSEUM OF FINE ART, BOSTON, MASSACHUSETTS
The museum's exhibits allow visitors to examine burial customs from Ancient Egypt to Roman times through:
• elaborately painted sarcophagus and canopic jars
• a large display of human and animal mummies

BRITISH MUSEUM, LONDON, ENGLAND
This museum has the largest and most comprehensive collection of ancient Egyptian artifacts outside Cairo. Its exhibits include:
• impressive display of Egyptian mummies
• body of Lindow Man, preserved in a peat bog in Cheshire.

EGYPTIAN MUSEUM, CAIRO, EGYPT
A spectacular display of art and artifacts from ancient Egypt:
• Royal Mummy Room contains the mummies of Tuthmosis II, Seti I, Ramses II, and other legendary pharaohs
• museum also houses the Tutankhamun collection—around 1,700 treasures from the boy king's tomb.

MUMMIFICATION MUSEUM, LUXOR, EGYPT
Displays explain the ancient Egyptian process of mummification and include:
• intact mummy and coffin of Maseharti, a high priest and general from the 21st dynasty period
• embalming equipment, such as instruments for removing internal organs and items needed by the mummy on its journey to the afterlife
• collection of mummified cats and rams.

ROEMER-UND-PELIZAEUS MUSEUM, HILDESHEIM, GERMANY
One of the premier Egyptian collections in the world. Exhibits include:
• large collection of Egyptian mummies, mummy masks, and coffins
• mummies of cats, ibises, and a 12-ft (3.5-m) long crocodile
• collection of mummy bundles and other artifacts from Peru.

USEFUL WEB SITES

• Ancient Egypt site run by the British Museum:
  www.ancientegypt.co.uk
• Mummies and how they were made:
  www.si.edu/resource/faq/nmnh/mummies.htm
• Maps and plans of tombs in the Valley of the Kings:
  www.friesian.com/tombs.htm
• Games and a map showing where mummies have been found:
  dsc.discovery.com/convergence/mummies/mummies.html
• Site about mummies and the Egyptian afterlife:
  www.si.umich.edu/CHICO/mummy/

Death mask from a Chimu mummy bundle

The Roxie Walker Gallery at the British Museum in London

Glossary

AFTERLIFE Life after death

AMULET A charm that the ancient Egyptians believed had magical powers to protect the body from evil or bring good luck. Amulets often took the form of plants, animals, or parts of the human body.

APIS BULL A sacred bull, which the ancient Egyptian believed was an incarnation of the god Ptah. When the Apis Bull died, its body was mummified and buried in a special tomb called the Serapeum.

ARCHAEOLOGIST A person who studies human history by excavating ancient sites and analyzing the buildings and remains found there

ARSENIC Short for arsenic trioxide, a white powdery substance that is highly poisonous

ATEF CROWN A crown topped with two large feathers, which was one of the symbols of the Egyptian god Osiris

AUTOPSY A scientific examination of a dead body, often to find out how the person died

BA In ancient Egypt, one form of a dead person's spirit, often pictured as a bird with a human head

BACTERIA Tiny microorganisms that cause some diseases and make dead bodies decay.

BOG A stretch of wet, spongy ground. Dead bodies can be naturally mummified in some types of bog because bogs contain little oxygen and this stops the growth of bacteria that normally decay bodies.

BOOK OF THE DEAD In ancient Egypt, a collection of magic spells that were painted inside coffins or on a roll of papyrus left in a tomb. These spells were intended to help the dead person on his or her perilous journey to the next world.

BOTANIST A scientist who studies plants

Statue of an Apis Bull

CACHE A hiding place for treasure. In Egyptology, the word is used to describe the secret hiding places where some royal mummies were concealed after their tombs in the Valley of the Kings had been looted by robbers.

CANOPIC JAR A jar with a lid in the shape of a god's head. Canopic jars were used to store the embalmed internal organs from an Egyptian mummy.

CARTONNAGE A material similar to papier mâché, made from scraps of linen or papyrus, stuck together with plaster or resin. In ancient Egypt, cartonnage was sometimes used to make mummy cases and mummy masks.

CARTOUCHE In ancient Egyptian writing, an oval shape containing the hieroglyphs that spelled out a pharaoh's name.

CATACOMB An underground cemetery, often in the form of a series of tunnels with recesses used as tombs.

CAT SCAN A scan, similar to an x-ray, but which produces a three-dimensional image of an object. CAT is short for Computerized Axial Tomography.

DJED PILLAR An amulet in the shape of a pillar. It was the symbol of the Egyptian god Osiris and represented survival, stability, and the possibility of life after death.

DNA Short for deoxyribonucleic acid, a material which is present in all living organisms and carries their genetic information.

DYNASTY A succesion, or family, of kings who are related to one another. Historians divide the long list of Egyptian pharaohs into 30 dynasties.

EMBALMING A chemical process used to preserve a dead body and stop it from decaying.

EXPOSURE Death caused by being exposed to severe weather conditions, such as extreme wind and cold

FAIENCE A form of decorated and glazed pottery

FORENSICS The application of biochemical and other scientific techniques to the investigation of crime. Forensic experts sometimes examine mummies to find out how they died.

FREEZE-DRIED Dried out by very cold weather conditions.

GIRDLE OF ISIS An amulet in the shape of a knot of cloth. It was the symbol of the Egyptian goddess Isis and represented her protective powers.

GLACIER A river of ice, which is slowly moving forward or retreating

GULLY A ravine or channel that has been worn away by water

HIEROGLYPHICS The form of writing used by the ancient Egyptians, in which pictures were used to represent words, syllables, or sounds

KA In ancient Egypt, one form of a person's spirit

KOHL A type of eye makeup used by the ancient Egyptians; a black powder used to outline the eyes, similar to modern-day eyeliner

LATE PERIOD The period of ancient Egyptian history that lasted from approximately 715 to 332 BCE

MIDDLE KINGDOM The period of ancient Egyptian history that lasted from approximately 2055 to 1650 BCE

A model of DNA

A djed pillar

A glacier

Scarab

MUMMIFORM In the shape of a mummy. The word is often used to describe the mummy-shaped coffins in which some Egyptians were buried.

MUMMY CASE A form of coffin, often made of wood or cartonnage, used to contain a mummified body

MUMMY MASK A mask representing the face of the dead person, which was placed over a mummy's face

NATRON A naturally occuring form of salt, found in dried lake beds. The Egyptians used natron to dry out a dead body before it was mummified.

NEMES HEADDRESS A distinctive, striped headdress of cloth folded over the hair, worn only by the Egyptian pharaoh

NEW KINGDOM The period of ancient Egyptian history which lasted from approximately 1550 to 1069 BCE

NOMADS People who have no settled home but who wander from place to place in search of fresh pasture for their animals

OLD KINGDOM The period of ancient Egyptian history that lasted from approximately 2686 to 2181 BCE

PAPYRUS A material for writing on, used by the ancient Egyptians. It was made from strips of reed woven together and beaten to form long rolls like paper.

PEAT A brown deposit, similar to soil, formed from partly decomposed plants. Peat can be burned as a fuel.

PECTORAL An ornament or piece of jewelry that is worn on the chest. A pectoral was sometimes enclosed in an Egyptian mummy's bandages.

PHARAOH The ruler of ancient Egypt. The Egyptians believed that the pharaoh was a living incarnation of the god Horus, so he was treated with great respect.

QUIVER A bag in which an archer stored his spare arrows

RADIOCARBON DATING A technique for finding the age of an organic object by measuring the amount of carbon-14 it contains. It can be used to date things such as dead bodies or ancient plant remains.

RADIOGRAPHER A person who takes x-ray pictures or operates an MRI or CAT scanner.

RISHI Decorated with a feather design; comes from the Arabic word for "feathered"

An Egyptian document, written on papyrus

SAND BURIAL An early form of burial used in ancient Egypt, in which the dead body was buried in the desert sand. The dry sand stopped the process of decay and mummified the body naturally by drying it out.

SARCOPHAGUS A coffin made of stone. In ancient Egypt a sarcophagus was usually a stone box, into which the mummy in its coffin was placed. The name means "flesh eater" in Greek.

SCARAB An Egyptian amulet in the shape of a beetle.

SHABTI A small model figure of a servant or worker. The ancient Egyptians believed that in the afterlife they might be required to do hard manual labor. Wealthy people were buried with shabti figures, who they believed would come to life and do this work for them.

SHRINE A casket or box containing sacred relics. In Egyptology, the word is used to describe one of a nest of boxes in which a pharaoh's coffin was placed.

SHROUD A large sheet of material used to wrap a dead body.

TANNING A process normally used to turn animal hides into leather by soaking them in a liquid containing tannic acid. Some bog mummies have also been tanned to preserve them

Wedjat eye

VALLEY OF THE KINGS A secluded valley across the Nile from the town of Thebes, where many Egyptian pharaohs were buried in hidden tombs.

VITAL ORGANS Organs, such as the heart and brain, which are essential for keeping the body alive.

WEDJAT EYE An eye symbol believed to protect a mummy's health and give the body new vitality. It represented the eye of the god Horus, which was miraculously restored after he lost it in a fight with evil.

XERORADIOGRAPH A form of x-ray image which emphasizes edges, so that the outlines of shapes are easier to see.

Index

Acknowledgments

The publisher would like to thank:
The staff of the Department of Egyptian Antiquities, British Museum, London, in particular John Taylor and Carole Andrews; Ian Mackay at the Museum of Mankind, London; Angela Thomas and Arthur Boulton of the Bolton Museum; John Saunders, Stephen Hughes, and the staff of the Department of Medical Physics, St. Thomas' Hospital, London (p. 51); Reg Davis; Don Brothwell; Joyce Filer; Guita Elmenteuse; George Bankes at the University of Manchester; Theya Molleson at the Natural History Museum, London; the Seventh Earl of Carnavon; the Egypt Exploration Society; Nicholas Reeves; William and Miranda MacQuitty; Peter Nahun; Martin Davies; Maria Demosthenous; Mitsuko Miyazaki in Japan; Martin Atcherley in Germany; Michael Dunning and Geoff Brightling for additional photography; Gillie Newman for illustrations on pp. 10 and 15; James Putnam for the illustration on p. 25; Belinda Rasmussen; Helena Spiteri for editorial help; Sharon Spencer and Manisha Patel for design help; Céline Carez for her enthusiastic research.

Picture credits
a=above, b=below, c=center, l=left, r=right
Ancient Art and Architecture Collection: 56cr; Ancient Egypt Picture Library: 68bl; Ardea, London Ltd: 23ac; /Akelindau: 13br; /John Mason: 44bc; /Peter Steyn: 45ar; Owen Beattie /University of Alberta: 9br; Birmingham Museum 64tl; British Museum: 23al, 28al, 29ar, 29br, 31br, 31ac, 34ar, 44ar, 59al, 59ar, 62bl, 64bl, 69bl, 71 bl, 71br; /Robert Harding Picture Library: 11br; Jean-Loup Charmet: 36al; Chief Constable of Cheshire: 58al; Christopher Cormack/Impact: 60al, 60ar, 60c, 60b, 61l, 61ar, 61cr, 61br; Corbis: 67tl, 67bl, 68cl; Reg Davis: 49al, 50al; C. M. Dixon: 63c; Alistair Duncan 64tr; Egyptian National Museum, Cairo /Giraudon /Bridgeman Art Library, London: 38cl; Egypt Tourist Office: 15bc; Electa, Milan: 6cr; E. T. archive: 29al; Mary Evans Picture Library: 14ar, 17br, 29bcl, 36bl, 39c, 40al, 41cl; Forhistorisk Museum, Moesgard: 58b; Ronald Grant Archive: 40bc, 68br; Griffith Institute, Ashmolean Museum, Oxford: 24al, 35cb, 38br; Hammer Film Productions/Advertising Archives: 41al; Robert Harding Picture Library: 11al, 29acl, 38bl, 38c, 38ar, 39al, 39ar, 39br, 55al, 63ar; Michael Holford: 7cr, 29ac, 55ar; Hulton-Deutsch Collection: 16bl, 26br, 47cr; Louvre, Paris/Bridgeman Art Library, London: 11cr, 42al, /Giraudon/Bridgeman Art Library, London: 13ar, /Photo R.M.N: 10cl, 25al, 42bl; MacQuitty Collection: 7br, 10ar; Manchester Museum, University of Manchester: 48b, 70br; Mansell Collection: 6ar, 10bl; Musée de l'Homme, Paris: 54br; Museum of London: 9bl; National Museum, Copenhagen: 58ar; National Museum, Greenland: 7c, 62-63b; Oldham Art Gallery, Lancs/Bridgeman Art Library, London: 43bc; ™ & © Lucasfilm Ltd. (LFL) 1981. All rights reserved. Courtesy of Lucasfilm Ltd./BFI Stills: 41tr; Pelizaeus-Museum, Hildesheim: 10tc, 12br, 14b; Popperfoto: 55c; 67cr; Rex Features Ltd: 6cl, 56bl, 56c, 57ar, 63acl; Photo R.M.N: 27c; Science Photo Library: David Nunuk 66bl; Silkeborg Museum, Denmark: 9cl; Sygma: 36br, 38al, 50ar, 51bl, 56al, 57al, 56-57b; University College, London: 62ar; Collection Viollet 11ar; Werner Forman Archive: /Dallas Museum of Art, USA 69br; /The Greenland Museum 66br; Xinhua News Agency: 63ac.
Jacket images: Front: Sandro Vannini/Corbis, b; British Museum, London, UK, t. Back: Musée De L'homme, Paris, l.